HISTORY AND UTOPIA

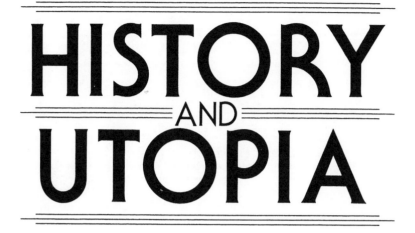

E. M. Cioran

Translated from the French
by Richard Howard

Foreword by Eugene Thacker

T0088047

Arcade Publishing • New York

Arcade Publishing books may be purchased in bulk at special discounts for
sales promotion, corporate gifts, fund-raising, or educational purposes. Special
editions can also be created to specifications. For details, contact the Special Sales
Department, Arcade Publishing, 307 West 36th Street, 11th Floor,
New York, NY 10018 or arcade@skyhorsepublishing.com.

Arcade Publishing® is a registered trademark of Skyhorse Publishing, Inc.®, a
Delaware corporation.

The essays in this volume have appeared previously in the following publications:
"Letter to a Faraway Friend" in *TriQuarterly*, no. 11 (Winter 1968)
"Russia and the Virus of Liberty" in *The Mississippi Review* 43–44 (Fall 1986)
"Learning from the Tyrants" in *Southern Humanities Review* 20, no. 4 (Fall 1986)
"Odyssey of Rancor" in *Grand Street* (Spring 1986)
"Mechanism of Utopia" in *Grand Street* (Spring 1987)
"The Golden Age" in *Antaeus* 21–22 (Summer 1976)

Visit our website at www.arcadepub.com.

10 9 8 7 6 5 4 3

Library of Congress Cataloging-in-Publication Data is available on file.

Print ISBN: 978-1-62872-425-7
Ebook ISBN: 978-1-62872-466-0

Printed in China

HISTORY
AND
UTOPIA

By the same author:

Drawn & Quartered
The Trouble with Being Born
The Temptation to Exist

Contents

═══

Foreword vii

Letter to a Faraway Friend 1

Russia and the Virus of Liberty 21

Learning from the Tyrants 38

Odyssey of Rancor 57

Mechanism of Utopia 80

The Golden Age 99

FOREWORD
by Eugene Thacker

The desire for utopia is, arguably, as urgent and as necessary as the desire for history. They are the meaning-making activities through which we as human beings project ourselves back into the past and forward into the future. And yet, both are fabrications, products of human intellectual labor, forged and re-forged with all the solidity and assurance of fact. That is, until the drama is played out once again.

This is readily apparent for the person living in exile—especially that of a self-imposed exile. Removed from one context and transplanted into another, human affairs become uncanny, a familiar pantomime with different sets and different costumes. Such was the outlook of E. M. Cioran, the Romanian-born author who, in 1946, relocated to Paris, vowing never to return to Romania. Writing in a language not his own, cut off from friends and family, and immersed in a cosmopolitan culture he kept at arm's length, the young Cioran began to develop a style of writing that was—and still is—difficult to place, somewhere between philosophy and poetry, the confession and the rant, ecstatic nihilism and black humor.

Strange, then, that an author like Cioran would publish a book with the title *History and Utopia*. By its title alone, *History and Utopia*—published in 1960—announces itself as a book about politics, a book of its moment. But readers will be disappointed if they expect to find a plan for political action, a manifesto for a coming revolution, or even a commentary on current events. The book's sentiments are encapsulated one of the essays, entitled "Odyssey of Rancor": "The multiplication of our kind borders on the obscene; the duty to love them, on the preposterous."

Composed of essays written during the late 1950s, *History and Utopia* contains a fascinating range of registers, from the confessional opening chapter to the almost cosmic final chapter. Coursing through it all is Cioran's own brand of political pessimism, an indictment of utopia that itself becomes a strange kind of misanthropic utopia, a utopia without hope, in which "politics" always fails because it regards itself as an exclusively human-centric endeavor: "Viscerally inclined to systems, we ceaselessly construct them, especially in politics, domain of pseudoproblems, breeding ground of the bad philosopher who resides in each of us, a realm I would be exiled from for the most commonplace of reasons, a piece of evidence which is raised in my eyes to the rank of a revelation: *politics revolves uniquely around man.*"

Coming from Cioran, such a zooming-out of what we normally consider "politics" should not surprise us. From his early Romanian book *On the Heights of Despair* (1934), to his first book written in French, *A Short History of Decay* (1949), to his critical dismantling of existentialism *The Temptation to Exist* (1956), Cioran had, by the 1950s, become known as a thinker who refused to be allied with any doctrine, be it religious, philosophical, or political. Notorious for its stark, nihilistic indictments against humanity, Cioran's writing is a sustained practice of refusal. At the same time, *History and Utopia* is unique among Cioran's books in that it does deal directly with the political issues of his time, most presciently, the turbulence in Eastern Europe—particularly in Romania—and the broader historical ramifications of an ongoing Cold War for a rapidly modernizing West.

We should note, however, that in spite of its explicit references to political events, *History and Utopia* is not the sole "political" writing of Cioran. In 1936 a young, impassioned, and politicized Cioran published a book in Romanian entitled *The Transfiguration of Romania*. Part of Romania's "young generation" of intellectuals, Cioran was taken by the political extremism then sweeping through Bucharest. A confused and delirious piece of writing, *The Transfiguration of Romania* was Cioran's attempt to embrace a "militant mysticism" of the old world and the new, a heady mix of nationalistic zeal and apocalyptic renewal. Filled with romantic formulas for "criminal lucidity" and "messianic fury," the author's enthusiasm quickly led to disenchantment, accompanied by an all-encompassing resentment for all political systems, moderate or extreme, left or right. By the end of the war, Cioran had disavowed the book and ceased writing about current events altogether.

But it continued to haunt him for the rest of his life. In interviews, when asked about *The Transfiguration of Romania*, Cioran is by turns remorseful, disdainful, bitter. The estrangement from his own writing would prompt him to write the series of essays that would become *History and Utopia*. There were external reasons as well. The 1956 insurrection in Budapest, which Cioran witnessed from afar, was intensified in his correspondence with his friend and former schoolmate, the philosopher Constantin Noica, held for years as a political prisoner by the Soviet-backed regime. Their correspondence would be the basis for the opening chapter of *History and Utopia*, "Letter to a Faraway Friend."

The "letter" is indicative of the many conflicted voices that constitute *History and Utopia*. Continuing his practice of "writing against oneself," Cioran's prose slips between the personal and the political, unwilling to engage with the world but incapable of detaching himself from it: "I seem to myself, among civilized men, a kind of intruder, a troglodyte enamored of decrepitude, plunged into subversive prayers, victim of a panic that emanates not from a vision of the world but from the spasms of the flesh and the *tenebrae* of the blood." An Augustine without his faith, a Kierkegaard without his leap.

Cioran proposes nothing—and, perhaps, therein lies his "politics." Neither heroic nor tragic, nor even comedic—*History and Utopia* is the testimony of someone who has given up on politics because, in part, he has given up on the human—or at least the image of humanity that incessantly feeds the political machinations of both history and utopia. "How could it be otherwise on a planet where flesh propagates with the shamelessness of a scourge? Wherever we go, we come up against the human, a repulsive ubiquity before which we fall into stupor and revolt . . ." All that remains is this void of refusal, though it is, in Cioran's own words, "a void that affords plentitude, a fulfilling void."

Letter to
a Faraway Friend

From that country which was ours and now is no one's, you urge me, after so many years of silence, to send you details about my occupations, and about this "wonderful" world in which, you say, I am lucky enough to live and move and have my being. I might answer that I am a man without occupation, and that this world is not in the least wonderful. But so laconic a reply cannot, for all its exactitude, assuage your curiosity or satisfy the many questions you raise. There is one among them which, scarcely to be distinguished from a reproach, strikes me more than all the rest: you ask if I ever intend to return to our own language, or if I shall remain faithful to this other tongue in which you (quite gratuitously) attribute to me a facility I do not, and never shall, possess. It would be the narrative of a nightmare, were I to give you a detailed account of the history of my relations with this borrowed idiom, with all these words so often weighed, worked over, refined, subtle to the point of non-existence, bowed beneath the exactions of nuance, inexpressive from having expressed everything, alarming in their precision, burdened with fatigue and modesty, discreet even in vulgarity. How should a Scyth come to terms with such terms, grasp their true meaning and wield them with scruple,

with probity? There is not one among them whose exhausted elegance fails to dizzy me: no longer a trace of earth,
of blood, of soul in such words. A syntax of severe, of
cadaverous dignity encompasses them and assigns them a
place from which God Himself could not dislodge them.
What consumption of coffee, of cigarettes, and of diction-
aries merely to write one halfway decent sentence in this
inapproachable language, too noble and too distinguished
for my taste! I realized as much, unfortunately, only after
the fact, when it was too late to change my course; otherwise
I should never have abandoned our own, whose odor of
growth and corruption I occasionally regret, that mixture
of sun and dung with all its nostalgic ugliness, its splendid
squalor. Return to it, I cannot; the tongue I was obliged to
adopt pinions and subjugates me by the very pains it has
cost me. Am I a "renegade," as you insinuate? "A man's
country is but a camp in the desert," says a Tibetan text. I
do not go so far and would give all the landscapes of the
world for that of my childhood. Yet I must add that, if I
make it into a paradise, the legerdemain or the infirmities
of my memory are exclusively responsible. Pursued by our
origins—we all are; the emotion mine inspire necessarily
translates itself into negative terms, the language of self-
punishment, of humiliation acknowledged and proclaimed,
of an accession to disaster. Is such patriotism answerable to
psychiatry? Perhaps, yet I cannot conceive of any other,
and, considering our destinies, it seems to me—why hide
it from you?—the only reasonable kind.

More fortunate than I, you have resigned yourself to our
natal dust; you possess, further, the faculty of enduring any
regime, including the most rigid varieties. Not that you lack
a nostalgia for caprice and chaos, but after all I know no

mind more refractory than yours to the superstitions of "democracy." There was a time, it is true, when I resisted it as much as you do, perhaps more than you do: I was young and could not admit other truths than mine, or concede to an adversary the right to possess, to exercise, to impose his own. That "sides," parties, could face yet not confound each other was beyond my comprehension. Shame of the Race, symbol of an anemic humanity without passions or convictions, unfit for absolutes, unworthy of a future, limited at every point, incapable of raising itself to the lofty wisdom which taught me that the object of an argument was the pulverization of the adversary—so I regarded the parliamentary system. Those regimes, on the other hand, that sought to eliminate and replace it seemed to me splendid without exception, in harmony with the movement of Life, my divinity in those days. If a man has not, by the time he is thirty, yielded to the fascination of every form of extremism—I don't know whether he is to be admired or scorned, regarded as a saint or a corpse. Lacking biological resources, has he not located himself above or below time? Positive *or* negative, the deficiency is no more than that. With neither the desire nor the will to destroy, he is suspect, he has triumphed over the demon or, more serious still, was never possessed by one. *To live* in any true sense of the word is to reject others; to accept them, one must be able to renounce, to do oneself violence, to act against one's own nature, to *weaken oneself*; we conceive freedom only for ourselves—we extend it to our neighbors only at the cost of exhausting efforts; whence the precariousness of liberalism, a defiance of our instincts, a brief and miraculous success, a state of exception, at the antipodes of our deepest imperatives. By our nature we are unsuited to it: only the

debilitation of our forces makes us accessible to it: tragedy
of a race which must debase itself on one hand to be en-
nobled on the other, and of which no member, unless by a
precocious decrepitude, sacrifices to "humane" principles.
Tolerance, the function of an extinguished ardor, of a disequilibrium resulting not from an excess but from a dearth
of energy—tolerance cannot seduce the young. We do not
involve ourselves in political struggles with impunity; it is
to the cult of which the young were the object that our age
owes its bloodthirsty aspect: the century's convulsions em-
anate from them, from their readiness to espouse an aberration and to translate it into action. Give them the hope
or the occasion of a massacre, they will follow you blindly.
At the end of adolescence, a man is a fanatic by definition;
I have been one myself, and to the limits of absurdity. Do
you remember that period when I poured out incendiary
tirades, less from a love of scandal than a longing to escape
a fever which, without the outlet of verbal dementia, would
certainly have consumed me? Convinced that the evils of
our society derived from *old men*, I conceived a liquidation
of every citizen over the age of forty, that onset of sclerosis
and mummification, that turning point after which, I chose
to believe, every individual becomes an insult to the nation
and a burden to the collectivity. So admirable did the project
seem to me that I did not hesitate to divulge it; those concerned were something less than appreciative of its tenor
and labeled me a cannibal: my career as a public benefactor
began under discouraging auspices. You yourself, though
so generous and, in your way, so enterprising, by dint of
reservations and objections had persuaded me to give it up.
Was my project so blameworthy? It merely expressed what
every man who loves his country hopes for in his inmost
heart: the suppression of half his compatriots.

When I think of those moments of enthusiasm and frenzy, of the wild speculations that raddled and ravaged my mind, I attribute them now not to dreams of philanthropy and destruction, to the obsession with some unascertainable purity, but to an animal melancholy which, concealed beneath the mask of fervor, functioned at my expense though I was its willing accomplice, enchanted not to be obliged, like so many others, to choose between the insipid and the atrocious. The atrocious falling to my portion, what more could I ask? I had a wolf's soul, and my ferocity, feeding on itself, satiated, flattered me: I was, in other words, the happiest of lycanthropes. Glory I aspired to and shunned in one and the same movement: once achieved, what is it worth, I reminded myself, from the moment it singles us out and imposes us only on the present and future generations, excludes us from the past? What is the use of being known, if we have not been so to this sage or that madman, to a Marcus Aurelius or to a Nero? We shall never have existed for so many of our idols, our name will have troubled none of the centuries *before* us; and those that come after—what do they matter? What does the future, that half of time, matter to the man who is infatuated with eternity?

By what struggles I managed to rid myself of such madness I shall not tell you, it would take too long, requiring one of those endless conversations that is, or was, a Balkan secret. Whatever my difficulties, they were far from being the sole cause of the change in my orientation; a more natural and more painful phenomenon greatly contributed to this: age, with its unmistakable symptoms. I began to show more and more signs of tolerance, symptoms, it seemed to me, of some inner upheaval, some doubtless incurable disease. Worst of all I no longer had the strength to desire my enemy's death; quite the contrary, I *understood* him, compared his venom to my own: he existed and—nameless downfall!—I was glad he existed. My hatreds, the source of my exultations, died down, diminished from day to day, and in departing carried off with them the best of myself. What will I do? Into what abyss will I creep? I kept wondering. And in proportion as my energy waned, my penchant for tolerance waxed; no doubt about it, I was no longer young: *others* seemed conceivable to me, even real. I said farewell to *The Ego and Its Own*; discretion tempted me: was I done for? One must be, in order to become a *sincere* democrat. To my delight, I realized that such was not exactly my case, that I retained certain vestiges of fanaticism, some traces of youth: I compromised none of my new principles, I was an *intractable* liberal. I am still. O happy incompatibility, O saving absurdity! I sometimes aspire to set an example as a perfect moderate: I congratulate myself at the same time upon not succeeding, so greatly do I fear my own dotage. The moment will come when, no longer fearing it, I shall approach that ideal equilibrium I sometimes dream of; and if, my friend, the years should lead you, as I hope, to a downfall like mine, then perhaps, toward the century's end, we shall sit side by side in our resuscitated parliament and, one as senile as the other, may both bear witness to a perpetual and enchanting spectacle. One becomes tolerant only insofar as one loses one's vigor, as one collapses—oh, charmingly!—into childhood, as one is too weary to torment others whether out of love or out of hatred.

As you see, I take "broad" views. So broad I have no idea where I stand on any problem at all. You shall judge as much for yourself; to the question you ask: "Do you still harbor your old prejudices against our little neighbor to the west, do you still resent her as much?" I don't know what answer to give; at best I can dumbfound or disappoint you. Because, of course, we do not have the same experience of Hungary.

Born beyond the Carpathians, you could not know the Hungarian policeman, terror of my Transylvanian childhood. When I so much as glimpsed one from afar, I was panic-stricken and ran away: he was the alien, the enemy; to hate was to hate *him*. Because of him, I abhorred all Hungarians with a truly Magyar passion. In other words they *interested* me. Subsequently, the circumstances having changed, I no longer had any reason to hate them. But the fact remains that long afterward I could not imagine an oppressor without evoking *their* defects, *their* glories. Who rebels, who rises in arms? Rarely the slave, but almost always the oppressor turned slave. The Hungarians know tyranny at close range, having wielded it with an incomparable proficiency: the minorities of the old monarchy could testify to that. Because they were so gifted, in their past, in the role of masters, they have been, in our own day, less disposed than any other nation of central Europe to endure slavery; if they had a talent for fiat, how could they fail to have one for freedom? Strong in their tradition as persecutors, accustomed to the mechanism of subjugation and intolerance, they have risen against a regime that has its similarities to the one they themselves had reserved for other peoples. But we, dear friend, not having had the occasion, hitherto, of being oppressors, cannot now have that of being rebels. Deprived of this double fortune, we bear our chains dutifully, and it would scarcely be gracious of me to deny the virtues of our discretion, the nobility of our servitude, while admitting nonetheless that the excesses of our modesty impel us to disturbing extremes; so much discretion exceeds all limits; it is so disproportionate that it sometimes manages to discourage me. I envy, then, the arrogance of our neighbors, I envy even their language, savage as it may be but of a beauty that has nothing human about it, with sonorities of another universe, powerful and corrosive, appropriate to prayer, to groans and to tears, risen out of hell to perpetuate its accent and its aura. Though I know only its swear words, Hungarian never fails to delight me, I never tire of hearing it, it enchants and repels me, I succumb to its charm and to its horror, to all those words of nectar and cyanide, so suited to the exigencies of an agony. It is in Hungarian that one should expire—or renounce dying.

The fact is, I hate my former masters less and less. Upon reflection, even in the days of their splendor, they were always alone in the heart of Europe, isolated in their pride and their regrets, lacking any profound affinities with the other nations. After several incursions into the West, where they could exhibit and expend their first savagery, they fell back, conquerors degenerating into sedentaries, to the banks of the Danube, there to sing, to lament, to erode their instincts. There is, in these refined Huns, a melancholy consisting of a suppressed cruelty, whose equivalent is not to be found elsewhere: it is as if the blood began dreaming about itself. And at last resolved itself into melody. Close to their essence, though defiled and even branded by civilization, conscious of descending from a unique horde, stamped by a fatuousness both profound and theatrical which affords them a style more romantic than tragic, how could they disappoint the mission that fell to their lot in the modern world: to rehabilitate chauvinism, by introducing into it enough pomp and fatality to make it picturesque to the eyes of the disabused observer. I am all the more inclined

to acknowledge their merits since it is they who have made
me suffer the worst humiliation, that of being born a serf,
as well as "pangs of shame"—the most intolerable of all,
according to one moralist. Have you yourself not experienced the voluptuous pleasure to be taken in an effort of
objectivity toward those who have flouted, scorned, mistreated you, especially when you secretly share their vices
and their miseries? Do not, from this, infer that I long to
be promoted to the rank of Magyar. I am far from any such
presumption: I know my limits and intend to abide by them.
On the other hand, I also know those of our neighbor, and
should my enthusiasm for her drop, even one degree, it
would suffice to disengage my vanity from the honor Hungary did me by persecuting me.

Peoples, much more than individuals, inspire contradictory sentiments; we love and loathe them at the same time;
objects of attachment and of aversion, they do not deserve
our harboring, in their behalf, a specific passion. Your par-
tiality to those of the West, whose defects you do not clearly
distinguish, is the effect of distance: an error of optics, or
a nostalgia for the inaccessible. Nor do you distinguish any
better the lacunae of bourgeois society; I even suspect you
of a certain leniency in its regard. That from such a distance
you should have a wonder-working view of it is natural
enough; since I know it at close range, it is my duty to
combat the illusions you may entertain. Not that such a
society is entirely and absolutely displeasing to me—you
know my weakness for the horrible—but the expenditure
of insensitivity it requires in order to be endured is out of
all proportion to my reserves of cynicism. It is an under-
statement to say that in this society injustices abound: in
truth, it is itself the quintessence of injustice. Only the idle,

the parasite, the expert in turpitude, the great swindler, and the petty crook profit by the benefits it bestows, the opulence on which it prides itself: surface pleasures and surface profusions. Under the shellac it shows off lies a world of desolation whose details I shall spare you. Without the intervention of a miracle, how explain that it does not reduce itself to dust before our eyes, or that someone does not blow it up instantaneously?

"Ours is worth no more; quite the contrary," you will object. I agree. But there's the rub! We find ourselves dealing with two types of society—both intolerable. And the worst of it is that the abuses in yours permit this one to persevere in its own, to offer its own horrors as a counterpoise to those cultivated *chez vous*. The capital reproach one can address to your regime is that it has ruined Utopia, a principle of renewal in both institutions and peoples. The bourgeoisie has understood the advantage to be derived from this failure against the adversaries of the status quo; the "miracle" which saves, which preserves it from an immediate destruction, is precisely the debacle of the other side, the spectacle of a great idea disfigured, the resulting disappointment which, laying hold of men's minds, paralyzes them. A really unhoped-for disappointment, a providential support for the bourgeois who lives on it and from it extracts the reason for his security. The masses are not stirred if they have no more than a choice between present evils and evils to come; resigned to those they suffer now, they have no interest in risking themselves in the direction of others which are unknown but certain. Foreseeable miseries do not excite men's imaginations, and there is no example of a revolution breaking out in the name of a dark future, a grim prophecy. Who could have guessed, in the last century, that the new society would, by its vices and its iniquities, permit the old one to preserve, even to consolidate itself; that the possible, having become reality, would fly to the rescue of the past?

On either side, we are at a nodal point, both fallen from that naïveté in which speculations on the future are elaborated. In the long run, life without utopia is suffocating, for the multitude at least: threatened otherwise with petrifaction, the world must have a new madness. This is the one piece of evidence to be gained from an analysis of the present. Meanwhile, our situation on this side is certainly a curious one. Imagine a society overpopulated with doubts; in which, with the exception of a few *strays*, no one adheres utterly to anything; in which, unscathed by superstitions and certainties, everyone pays lip service to freedom and no one respects the form of government that defends and incarnates it. Ideals without content, or, to use a word quite as adulterated, myths without substance. You are disappointed after promises that could not be kept; we, by a lack of any promises at all. At least we are aware of the advantage the intelligence gains from a regime that, for the moment, lets it function as it will, without submitting it to the rigors of any imperative. The bourgeois believes in nothing, true enough; but this truth is, I daresay, the positive side of his vacuum, for freedom can be manifested only in the void of beliefs, in the absence of axioms, and only where the laws have no more authority than a hypothesis. If you were to object that the bourgeois nonetheless believes in something, that money perfectly fulfills, for him, the function of a dogma, I should reply that this worst of all dogmas is, strange as it may seem, the one that is the most endurable for the mind. We forgive others their wealth if, in exchange, they let us starve to death *in our own way.* No, it is not so sinister, this society which pays no attention to you, which abandons you, guarantees you the right to attack it, invites you, even obliges you to do so in its hours of sloth when it lacks energy to execrate itself. As indifferent, in the last instance, to its own fate as to yours, it is in no way eager to infringe upon your misfortunes, neither to reduce nor to aggravate them, and if it exploits you, it does so by an automatism, without premeditation or spite, as is appropriate to weary and satiated brutes that are as contaminated by skepticism as their victims. The difference between regimes is less important than it appears; you are alone by force, we without constraint. Is the gap so wide between an inferno and a ravaging paradise? All societies are bad; but there are degrees, I admit, and if I have chosen this one, it is because I can distinguish among the nuances of trumpery.

Freedom, I was saying, demands, in order to manifest itself, a vacuum; it requires a void—and succumbs to it. The condition that determines it is the very one that annihilates it. It lacks foundations; the more complete it is, the more it overhangs an abyss, for everything threatens it, down to the principle from which it derives. Man is so little made to endure or deserve it, that the very benefits he receives from it crush him, and freedom ultimately burdens him to the point where he prefers, to its excesses, those of terror. To these disadvantages are added others: a liberal society, eliminating "mystery," "the absolute," "order," and possessing a true metaphysic no more than a true police, casts the individual back upon himself, while dividing him from what he is, from his own depths. If such a society lacks roots, if it is essentially *superficial,* this is because freedom, fragile in itself, has no means of maintaining itself, of sur-

viving the dangers which threaten it from without and from
within; it appears, moreover, only in the twilight of a regime,
only at the moment when a class is declining, dissolving: it
was the collapse of the aristocracy that allowed the eigh-
teenth century to divagate so magnificently; it is the collapse
of the bourgeoisie that allows us today to cultivate our fan-
tasies. Freedoms prosper only in a sick body politic: tolerance and impotence are synonyms. This is patent in politics
as everywhere else. When I first glimpsed this truth, the
earth gave way under my feet. Even now, though I tell
myself: "You belong to a society of free men," the pride I
take in the fact is still accompanied by a sense of dread and
inanity, the result of my terrible certitude. In the course of
history, freedom occupies no more instants than ecstasy in
the life of a mystic. It escapes us at the very moment we
try to grasp and formulate it: no one can enjoy freedom
without trembling. Desperately mortal, once it is established
it postulates its lack of a future and labors on, with all its
undermined forces, to its own negation, its own agony. Is
there not a certain perversion in our love for it? And is it
not horrifying to worship what neither can nor cares to *last*?
For you who no longer possess it, freedom is everything;
for us who do, it is merely an illusion, because we know
that we shall lose it and that, in any case, it is made to be
lost. Hence, at the heart of our void, we cast our glances in
all directions, without thereby neglecting the possibilities
of salvation that reside in ourselves. There is, moreover, no
such thing as a perfect vacuum in history. That unheard-of
absence to which we are reduced, and which I have the
pleasure and the misfortune to reveal to you, you would be
mistaken to imagine merely a blank, uninscribed; for in it
I discern—presentiment or hallucination?—a kind of ex-

pectation of *other gods*. Which ones? No one can say. All I know, and it is what everyone knows, is that a situation like ours cannot be endured indefinitely. Deep within our consciousness, one hope crucifies us, one apprehension exalts us. Unless they assent to death, the old nations, however rotten, cannot dispense with new idols. Whether or not the West is irremediably corrupt, it must rethink all the ideas stolen from it and applied (by counterfeiting them) elsewhere: I mean that it is incumbent upon the West, if it seeks to make itself illustrious once more by a throb or a vestige of honor, to take back the utopias that, in its need for comfort, it has abandoned to the others, thereby dispossessing itself of its genius and its mission. Whereas it was the West's duty to put communism into practice, to adjust it to its traditions, to humanize, liberalize, and thereafter propose it to the world, it has left to the East the privilege of realizing the unrealizable, of deriving power and prestige from the finest of our modern illusions. In the battle of ideologies, the West has shown itself timid, harmless; some congratulate it for this, whereas it is to be blamed: in our day and age, one does not accede to hegemony without the cooperation of those lofty, lying principles employed by virile peoples to dissimulate their instincts and their aims. Having abandoned reality for ideas, and ideas for ideology, man has slid toward a derived universe, toward a world of subproducts in which fiction acquires the virtues of a primordial datum. This process is the fruit of all the rebellions and all the heresies of the West, yet the West refuses to draw the final consequences: it has not initiated the revolution that was its imperative, the revolution that its entire past demanded, nor has it carried to their conclusion the upheavals of which it was the instigator. By disinheriting itself in favor of its enemies, the West risks compromising its denouement and missing a supreme opportunity. Not content with having betrayed all those precursors, all those schismatics who have prepared and formed it from Luther to Marx, it still supposes that someone will come, from the outside, to initiate *its* revolution, to bring back its utopias and its dreams. Will the West ever understand that it has a political destiny and a role only if it rediscovers in itself its old dreams and its old utopias, as well as the lies of its old pride? For the moment, it is the adversaries of the West who, converted into theoreticians of the duty it evades, are building their empires on its timidity, its lassitude. What curse has fallen upon it that at the term of its trajectory it produces only these businessmen, these shopkeepers, these racketeers with their blank stares and atrophied smiles, to be met with everywhere, in Italy as in France, in England as in Germany? Is it with such vermin as this that a civilization so delicate and so complex must come to an end? Perhaps we had to endure this, out of abjection, in order to be able to conceive of another kind of man. As a good liberal, I do not want to carry indignation to the point of intolerance or to let myself be carried away by my moods, though it is sweet, for us all, to be able to infringe upon the principles that appeal to our generosity. I merely wanted to point out to you that our world, far from wonderful, could in a sense become so if it consented not to annihilate itself (as it inclines all too readily to do), but to liquidate its failures by undertaking *impossible* tasks, opposed to that dreadful good sense which is disfiguring and destroying it today.

The feelings the West inspires in me are no less mixed than those I entertain toward my country, toward Hungary, or toward our *big* neighbor, whose indiscreet proximity you are in a better position to appreciate than I. The excessive good and bad I think of Russia, the impressions she suggests when I reflect upon her destiny—how can I put such things without falling into the preposterous? I make no claim to change your opinion about her, I merely want you to know what she represents for me and what place she occupies among my obsessions. The more I think about her, the more I find that Russia has formed herself, down through the ages, not the way a nation is formed, but the way a universe is formed, the moments of her evolution participating less in history than in a somber, terrifying cosmogony. Those tsars with their look of dried-up divinities, giants solicited by sanctity and crime, collapsing into prayer and panic—they were, as are these recent tyrants who have replaced them, closer to a geological vitality than to human anemia, despots perpetuating in our time the primordial sap, the primordial spoilage, and triumphing over us all by their inexhaustible reserves of chaos. Crowned or not, it was their significance, as it is still, to leap *beyond civilization*, to engulf it if need be; the operation was inscribed within their nature, since they have always suffered from the same obsession: to extend their supremacy over our dreams and our rebellions, to constitute an empire as vast as our disappointments or our dreads. Such a nation, coterminous both in its thoughts and in its actions with the confines of the globe, does not measure itself by present standards or explain itself in ordinary terms, in an intelligible language: it would require the jargon of the Gnostics, enriched by that of a general paralysis. Certainly it borders (has not Rilke assured us?) on God; as it also does, unfortunately, on our own country, and will again, in a more or less immediate future, on many others—I dare not say on all, despite the specific warnings that a malignant prescience intimates. Wherever we are, Russia already touches us, if not geographically, then without a doubt internally. I am more disposed than any man I know to acknowledge my debts to her: without her writers, would I ever have grown aware of my wounds and of my duty to surrender to them? Without her and without them, would I not have wasted my agonies, missed out on my chaos? This penchant which leads me to make an impartial judgment upon her and at the same time to testify to my gratitude is hardly, I fear, to your taste at the present time. I therefore break off such unseasonable eulogies, stuffing them inside myself where they will be condemned to be fruitful and multiply.

Even in the days when we amused ourselves by tallying our agreements and our differences, you reproached me for my mania of judging without bias both what I take to heart and what I execrate, of entertaining only double—necessarily false—feelings which you imputed to my incapacity to experience a true passion, while insisting on the delights I derive from them. Your diagnosis was not inexact; yet you erred with regard to the category of the delights. Do you suppose it is so agreeable to be both idolater and victim of the pro and the con, an enthusiast divided against his enthusiasms, a raving madman eager for *objectivity*? This does not happen without sufferings: the instincts protest, and it is indeed despite and against them that one advances toward an absolute irresolution, a state scarcely distinct from what the language of the ecstatics calls "the last point of annihilation." In order to know, myself, the whole of my thoughts about anything at all, in order to pronounce not only on a problem but on a trifle, I must oppose the major vice of my mind, that propensity to espouse all causes and at the same time dissociate myself from them, a kind of omnipresent virus divided between covetousness and satiety, a benign yet deadly agent as impatient as it is blasé, undecided between scourges, inept at adopting and specializing in *one*, shifting from each to the other without discrimination or effectiveness, bearer and bungler of the incurable, a traitor to all diseases, those of others as to its own.

Never to have occasion to take a position, to make up one's mind, or to define oneself—there is no wish I make more often. But we do not always master our moods, those attitudes in the bud, those rough drafts of theory. Viscerally inclined to systems, we ceaselessly construct them, especially in politics, domain of pseudoproblems, breeding grounds of the bad philosopher who resides in each of us, a realm I would be exiled from for the most commonplace of reasons, a piece of evidence which is raised in my eyes to the rank of a revelation: *politics revolves uniquely around man.* Having lost the taste for beings, I nonetheless wear myself out *in vain* acquiring one for things; necessarily limited to the interval that separates them, I expend and exhaust myself upon their shadow. Shadows too, these nations whose fate intrigues me, less for themselves than for the pretext they afford of revenging myself upon what has neither form nor outline, upon entities and symbols. The idler who loves violence safeguards his *savoir vivre* by confining himself in an abstract hell. Abandoning the individual, he frees himself of names and faces, deals with the imprecise, the general, and, orienting his thirst for exterminations to the impalpable, conceives a new genre: the pamphlet *without object.*

Clinging to fractions of ideas and to figments of dreams,

having arrived at reflection by accident or by hysteria, and not at all by a concern for rigor, I seem to myself, among civilized men, a kind of intruder, a troglodyte enamored of decrepitude, plunged into subversive prayers, victim of a panic that emanates not from a vision of the world but from the spasms of the flesh and the *tenebrae* of the blood. Impermeable to the solicitations of clarity and to the Latin contamination, I feel Asia stirring in my veins: am I the offspring of some inadmissible tribe, or the spokesman of a race once turbulent, today mute? Often the temptation seizes me to forge for myself another genealogy, to *change* ancestors, to choose among those who, in their day, spread grief among the nations, contrary to my own, to our modest and martyred land stuffed with miseries, amalgamated to the mud and groaning beneath the anathema of the ages. Yes, in my crises of fatuity, I incline to believe myself the epigone of some horde illustrious for its depredations, a Turanian at heart, legitimate heir of the steppes, the last Mongol. . . .

I would not end here without once again warning you against the enthusiasm or the jealousy my "luck" inspires in you, specifically the opportunity to loll in a city whose memory doubtless haunts you, despite your roots in our evaporated country. This city, which I would exchange for no other in the world, is for that very reason the source of my misfortunes. All that is not Paris being equal in my eyes, I often regret that wars have spared it, that it has not perished like so many others. Destroyed, it would have rid me of the happiness of living here, I could have spent my days elsewhere, at the ends of the earth. I shall never forgive Paris for having bound me to space, for making me *from somewhere*. Mind you, I am not forgetting for a moment that four-fifths of its inhabitants, as Chamfort has already noted, "die of grief." I should add further, for your edification, that the remaining fifth, the privileged few of whom I am one, are no different in their feelings, and that they even envy that majority its advantage of knowing *of what* to die.

Russia and
the Virus of Liberty

Every country, I sometimes think, should be like Switzerland—should complacently subside into hygiene, insipidity, the worship of laws, and the cult of humanity; at other times I admire only nations untouched by scruple in thought or deed, feverish and insatiable, ever ready to devour others and themselves, riding roughshod over all values opposed to their ascent and their success, scornful of prudence, that plague of superannuated peoples weary of themselves as of all the rest and apparently captivated by the smell of mold.

In the same way, if I abominate tyrants, I nonetheless see that they constitute the warp of history, and that without them the idea or the course of an empire would be inconceivable. Superlatively odious, of an inspired bestiality, they suggest man driven to his limits, the ultimate exasperation of his turpitudes and his virtues. Ivan the Terrible, to cite only the most fascinating among them, exhausts every nook and cranny of psychology: as complex in his madness as in his politics, having made his reign, and to a certain degree his country, into a model nightmare, prototype of a perennial hallucination, a mixture of Mongolia and Byzantium, combining the qualities and the defects of a khan and a basileus, a monster of demoniac rages and sordid dejection,

torn between bloodthirstiness and remorse, his joviality enriched with taunts and crowned with sneers, he had a passion
for crime; as have we all, insofar as we exist: transgressions
against others or ourselves. Only in us it remains unslaked,
that passion, so that our works, whatever they may be, derive
from our incapacity to kill or to kill ourselves. We do not
always acknowledge as much, we are glad to ignore the cozy
mechanism of our infirmities. If I am obsessed by the tsars
or the Roman emperors, it is because such infirmities, concealed in us, show quite plainly in them. They reveal us to
ourselves, they incarnate and illustrate our secrets. I think
especially of those who, doomed to an awesome degener-
ation, turned on their own and, fearing to be loved by them,
sent them to their doom. They were powerful, yet they
were wretched, unsatiated by the terror of others. Are they
not a sort of projection of the evil genius that dwells in us
all and tempts us to believe we must leave nothing standing
around us? It is with such thoughts and such instincts that
an empire is formed: in it cooperates that subsoil of our
consciousness in which are hidden our dearest faults.

Emerging from unsoundable depths, possessed of an original
vitality, the ambition to rule the world appears only in certain individuals and at certain periods, without direct relation to the quality of the nation in which it is manifested:
the difference between Napoleon and Genghis Khan is less
than between the former and any French politician of the
subsequent republics. But these depths, like this impulse,
can be exhausted—can run dry.

Charlemagne, Frederick II von Hohenstaufen, Charles
V, Bonaparte, Hitler were tempted, each in his own way,
to realize the idea of universal empire; they failed to do so,

more or less fortunately. The West, where this idea no longer inspires anything but irony or uneasiness, now lives in shame of its conquests; but oddly enough, it is precisely when the West retreats that its formulas triumph and spread; turned against Western power and Western supremacy, they find an echo outside Western frontiers. The West wins by losing. This was how Greece prevailed in the realm of the mind, once she had ceased being a power and even a nation; her philosophy and her arts were pilfered, her productions won a certain victory, without her talents being assimilable; in the same way, the West is—will be—stripped of everything, except its genius. A civilization proves its fecundity by its talent to incite others to imitate it; when it no longer dazzles them, it is reduced to an epitome of vestiges and shards.

Abandoning this corner of the world, the notion of empire would find a providential climate in Russia, where it has always existed, moreover—singularly on the spiritual level. After the fall of Byzantium, Moscow became, for the Orthodox consciousness, the third Rome, heir of the "true" Christianity, the true faith. First messianic awakening. The second had to wait until our own day and age; but that awakening is due, this time, to the resignation of the West. In the fifteenth century, Russia profited by a religious void, as she profits today by a political one. Two major opportunities to absorb her historical responsibilities.

When Mahomet II lay siege to Constantinople, Christendom, divided as always and delighted, moreover, to have lost all memory of the Crusades, declined to intervene. At first the besieged city expressed a certain irritation which, as the disaster came into focus, turned to stupor. Oscillating between panic and a secret satisfaction, the pope promised aid, which came too late: what was the use of taking so much trouble for "schismatics"? The "schism," however, was to gain strength elsewhere. Did Rome prefer Moscow to Byzantium? A distant enemy is always preferable to the one at the gate. In the same way, in our own times, the British would opt for a Russian preponderance in Europe over a German one. Germany was *too close.*

Russia's claims to turn from vague primacy to distinct hegemony are not unfounded. What would have become of the West if she had not halted and absorbed the Mongol invasion? For over two centuries of humiliation and servitude, Russia was excluded from history, while the Western nations indulged themselves in the luxury of tearing each other to pieces. Had Russia been in a condition to develop unhampered, she would have become a first-rate power on the eve of modern times; what she is now she would have been in the sixteenth or seventeenth century. And the West? Perhaps today the West would be *Orthodox,* and Rome would enthrone not the Holy See but the Holy Synod. But the Russians can still catch up. If they manage, as there is every reason to expect, to execute their plans, it is not out of the question that they will arrange matters with the sovereign pontiff. Whether in the name of Marxism or of Orthodoxy, they are fated to foil the Church's authority and prestige— they cannot tolerate its aims without abdicating the essential point of their mission and their program. Under the tsars, identifying the Church with an instrument of Antichrist, they offered prayers *against it*; now, holding it to be a Satanic tool of Reaction, they overwhelm it with invectives rather more effective than their old anathemas; soon they will overcome it with all their weight and all their power.

And it is not at all impossible that our age may count among its curiosities, and in the form of a frivolous apocalypse, the disappearance of St. Peter's last successor.

By sanctifying History in order to discredit God, Marxism has merely rendered Him more peculiar and more haunting. You can stifle every impulse in humanity except the need for an Absolute, which will survive the destruction of temples and even the disappearance of religion on earth. The core of the Russian people being religious, they will inevitably gain the upper hand. Reasons of a historical order will have a good deal to do with this triumph.

By adopting Orthodoxy, Russia manifested her desire to stand apart from the West; it was her way of defining herself, from the start. Never, outside certain aristocratic circles, did she let herself be seduced by the Catholic—as it happened, Jesuit—missionaries. A schism does not express the divergencies of doctrine so much as a will to ethnic affirmation: what appears in it is less an abstract controversy than a national reflex. It was not the absurd question of the *filioque* that divided the churches: Byzantium wanted its total autonomy; Moscow a fortiori. Schisms and heresies are nationalisms in disguise. But whereas the Reformation merely assumed the appearance of a family quarrel, of a scandal *within* the West, Orthodox particularism, acquiring a more profound character, was to mark a division from the Western world itself. By rejecting Catholicism, Russia delayed her evolution, lost a crucial opportunity for civilizing herself rapidly, while gaining in substance and in unity; her stagnation rendered her *different*, made her *other*; this is what she aspired to, doubtless foreseeing that the West would one day regret its head start.

The stronger Russia became, the more aware she grew of her roots, from which, in some sense, Marxism will have alienated her; after a forced cure of universalism, she will re-Russify, in favor of Orthodoxy. And, moreover, she will have stamped Marxism with a distinctly Slavic character: Marxism enSlaved. . . . Any nation of a certain scope that adopts an ideology alien to its traditions will adapt and denature it, inflect it in the direction of its own national destiny, distort it to its own advantage, ultimately rendering it indistinguishable from its own genius. A people possesses a necessarily distorting optic all its own, a defect of vision which, far from disconcerting it, flatters and stimulates. . . . The truths it avails itself of, whatever they may lack in objective value, are nonetheless vital and produce, as such, the kinds of errors that constitute the diversity of the historical landscape, granted that the historian—skeptical by métier, temperament, and option—is stationed, from the start, outside of Truth.

While the Western nations exhausted themselves in their struggle for freedom and, still more, in that freedom once acquired (nothing is so wearing as the possession or the abuse of liberty), the Russian people was suffering without self-expenditure; for one expends oneself only in history, and since the Russians were excluded from history, they were obliged to submit to the infallible systems of despotism inflicted upon them: an obscure, vegetative existence which allowed them to gain strength, to accumulate energy, to amass reserves, and to draw from their servitude the maximum of biological advantage. In this, Orthodoxy was a great help—but a popular Orthodoxy, admirably articulated to keep that people apart from the course of events and opposed to the official Orthodoxy which oriented the govern-

ment toward imperialist aims. The double face of the
Orthodox Church: on the one hand it militated in favor of
the somnolence of the masses; on the other, as an auxiliary
of the tsars, it wakened popular ambitions and made possible
enormous conquests in the name of a passive population.
Fortunate passivity, which assured the Russians their present
predominance, fruit of their historical belatedness. Whether
favorable or hostile to them, all of Europe's enterprises
hinge on them; once she puts them at the heart of her
interests and her anxieties, she acknowledges that they have
the potential to dominate her. Thus is virtually realized one
of the Russians' oldest dreams. That they have attained it
under the auspices of an ideology of foreign provenance
adds the spice of a further paradox to their success. What
matters, finally, is that the regime be Russian, and entirely
in the traditions of the country. Is it not revealing that the
Revolution, a direct product of Occidentalist theories, was
increasingly oriented toward Slavophile ideas? Moreover, a
people represents not so much an aggregate of ideas and
theories as of *obsessions*: those of Russians, whatever their
political complexion, are always, if not identical, at least
related. A Tchaadaev who found no virtue in his country
or a Gogol who mocked it pitilessly was just as attached to
it as a Dostoevsky. The most extreme of the Nihilists, Net-
chaiev, was quite as obsessed by it as Pobiedonostsev, pro-
curator of the Holy Synod and a reactionary through and
through. Only this obsession counts. The rest is merely
attitude.

For Russia to adapt to a liberal regime, she would have to
weaken considerably—her vigor would have to decline; better still: she would have to lose her specific character and

denationalize in depth. How would she manage this, with her unbroached internal resources and her thousand years of autocracy? Even if she were to achieve such a thing in one bound, she would instantly disintegrate. Even more than a nation, an empire, if it is to survive and to flourish, requires a certain dose of terror. France herself could invest in democracy only when her springs were beginning to loosen, only when, no longer seeking hegemony, she was preparing to become prudent and respectable. Her First Empire was her final folly. Thereupon, accessible to liberty, she would become painfully accustomed to it, through a number of convulsions, unlike England, which—a bewildering example—had *free relations* of long standing, without shocks or dangers, thanks to the conformism and the enlightened stupidity of her citizens (the country has not produced, to my knowledge, a single anarchist).

In the long run, time favors the fettered nations which, amassing forces and illusions, live in the future, in hope; but what can be hoped for in freedom—or in the regime which incarnates it, constituted of dissipation, serenity, and spinelessness? A marvel that has nothing to offer, democracy is at once a nation's paradise and its tomb. Life has meaning only in democracy, yet she lacks life. . . . Immediate happiness, imminent disaster—inconsistency of a regime to which one does not adhere without falling on the horns of an agonizing dilemma.

Better furnished, more fortunate, Russia need not face such problems, absolute power being for her, as Karamzin already remarked, the "very basis of her being." Ever aspiring to freedom without ever attaining it—is this not her great superiority over the West, which, alas! has long since attained to it? Russia, moreover, is not ashamed of her empire; quite the contrary, she dreams only of extending it. Who more than Russia has hastened to profit by the acquisitions of other peoples? The achievements of Peter the Great, even those of the Revolution, participate in an *inspired parasitism*. And it is true that she endured even the horrors of the Tartar yoke with a certain ingenuity.

If, while confined in a calculated isolation, Russia has managed to imitate the West, she has managed even better to be admired by that West and to seduce some of its best minds. The Encyclopedists were infatuated by the schemes of Peter and Catherine, just as the heirs of the Enlightenment (I mean the Left) were to be infatuated with those of Lenin and Stalin. This phenomenon argues in favor of Russia, but not of the Westerners who, complicated and ravaged to the last degree and seeking "progress" elsewhere, outside themselves and their creations, today find themselves paradoxically closer to Dostoevsky's characters than do the Russians themselves. Yet we might observe that they evoke only the defeated aspects of these same characters, that they possess neither their ferocious obsessions nor their virile sulks: so many "possessed" men, weakened by ratiocination and scruples, eroded by subtle remorse, by a thousand interrogations, martyrs of doubt, dazzled and annihilated by their own perplexities. . . .

Each civilization believes that its way of life is the only right one and the only one conceivable—that it must convert the world to it or inflict it upon the world; its way of life is equivalent to an explicit or camouflaged soteriology; indeed, to an elegant imperialism, but one that ceases to be so as soon as it is accompanied by military enterprise. You do not found an empire by whim. You subjugate others so they will imitate you, so they will model themselves on you, on your beliefs and your habits; then comes the perverse imperative to make slaves out of them in order to contemplate therein the flattering or caricatural sketch of yourself. I grant that there is such a thing as a qualitative hierarchy of empires: the Mongols and the Romans did not subjugate peoples for the same reasons, and their conquests did not have the same result. It is nonetheless true that they were equally expert in doing away with their adversary *by reducing him to their own image.*

Whether she has provoked or suffered, then, Russia has never been content with mediocre misfortunes. The same will be true of her future: she will fall upon Europe by a physical fatality, by the automatism of her mass, by her superabundant and morbid vitality so propitious to the generation of an empire (in which a nation's megalomania is always materialized), by that health of hers, crammed with the unforeseen, with horrors and enigmas, allocated to the service of a messianic idea, rudiment and prefiguration of all conquests. When the Slavophiles asserted that Russia must *save* the world, they were employing a euphemism: one hardly saves a world without ruling it. As for a nation, it finds its life-principle in itself or nowhere: how would it be saved by another? Russia still thinks—secularizing the Slavophiles' language and their conception—that it is her task to ensure the world's safety, the West's first of all, toward which, moreover, she has never experienced a clearcut feeling, only attraction and repulsion, and jealousy (that jumble of secret worship and ostensible aversion) inspired by the spectacle of a corruption as enviable as it is dangerous, contact with which is to be sought—but still more to be shunned.

Reluctant to define himself and to accept limits, culti-
vating ambiguity in politics, in morals, and, more seriously,
in geography, with none of the naïvetés inherent in "civilized
men" rendered opaque to reality by the excesses of a ra-
tionalist tradition, the Russian, subtle by intuition as much
as by the age-old experience of dissimulation, is perhaps a
child historically, but in no case psychologically; whence his
complexity as a man of young instincts and old secrets—
whence too the contradictions, exacerbated to grotesquerie,
of his attitudes. When he decides to be profound (and he
succeeds quite effortlessly), he disfigures the slightest fact,
the merest idea. It is as if he has the mania of a monumental
grimace. Everything is dizzying, dreadful, and ineffable in
the history of his ideas, revolutionary or otherwise. He is
still an incorrigible amateur of utopias; now, utopia is the
grotesque en rose, the need to associate happiness—that is,
the improbable—with becoming, and to coerce an optimistic, aerial vision to the point where it rejoins its own source:
the very cynicism it sought to combat. In short, a monstrous
fantasy.

That Russia is in a position to realize her dream of a
universal empire is a likelihood but not a certitude; on the
other hand, it is patent that Russia can conquer and annex
all Europe, and even that she will proceed to do so, if only
to reassure the rest of the world. . . . She is content with so
little! Where to find a more convincing proof of modesty,
of moderation? The tip of a continent! Meanwhile, she con-
templates it with the same eye with which the Mongols
regarded China and the Turks Byzantium—with this difference, though, that she has already assimilated a good
many Western values, whereas the Tartar and Ottoman hordes
had only a wholly material superiority over their future prey.

It is doubtless regrettable that Russia has not passed through the Renaissance: all her inequalities derive from that. But with her gift for making up time, she will be, in a century, perhaps in less, as refined, as vulnerable as that post-Renaissance West, at a level of civilization that can be outdone only by *descending.* History's supreme ambition is to record the variations of this level. Russia's, inferior to that of Europe, can only rise, and Russia with it: which is as much as to say that she is doomed to ascent. By rising, however, does she not risk, unbridled as she is, losing her equilibrium, bursting into ruins? With her millions of souls kneaded by sects and by steppes, she gives a singular impression of space and of claustration, of immensity and of suffocation, of the North in short, but of a special North, one irreducible to our analyses, a North marked by a sleep and a hope that make us tremble, by a night rich in explosions, by a dawn we shall remember. No Mediterranean transparency and gratuitousness in these Hyperboreans whose past, like their present, seems to belong to a different *duration* from ours. Facing the West's fragility and renown, they experience an embarrassment, the consequence of their belated awakening and of their unemployed vigor: this is the inferiority complex *of the strong.* . . . They will escape it, they will overcome it. The sole point of light in our future is their nostalgia—so secret and so intense—for a delicate world of deliquescent charms. If they accede to it (as appears to be the obvious direction of their fate) they will be civilized at the expense of their instincts and—delightful prospect—they too will be infected with the virus of liberty.

The more humane an empire becomes, the more readily there develop within it the contradictions by which it will perish. Of composite demeanor, of heterogeneous structure (the converse of a nation, that organic reality), an empire requires, to subsist, the cohesive principle of terror. If it lays itself open to tolerance, that "virtue" will destroy its unity and its power, and will act upon it in the manner of a deadly poison it has administered to itself. This is because tolerance is not only the pseudonym of freedom, but also of mind; and mind, even more deadly to empires than to individuals, erodes them, compromises their solidity, and accelerates their collapse. Hence it is the very instrument an ironic providence employs to destroy them.

If, despite the arbitrariness of the attempt, we were to divert ourselves by establishing *zones of vitality* in Europe, we should discover that the farther east we move, the more evident *instinct* becomes, and the less noticeable as we head west. The Russians are far from possessing an exclusive claim to it, though even the other nations that possess instinct belong in varying degrees to the Soviet sphere of influence. These nations have not spoken their last word, far from it; some of them, like Poland or Hungary, have played a not negligible part in history; others, like Yugoslavia, Bulgaria, and Rumania, having lived in the shadows, have endured only short-lived convulsions. But whatever their past has been, and independently of their level of civilization, they all still possess a biological capital it would be futile to seek in the West. Mistreated, disinherited, cast into an anonymous martyrdom, pinioned between sloth and sedition, they may yet know a coming compensation for so many ordeals, so many humiliations, and even so many cowardices. The *degree of instinct* is not measured from outside; to determine its intensity, we must have frequented (or divined) these countries, the only ones in the world still to espouse, in their

splendid blindness, the destinies of the West. Imagine our
continent incorporated into the Russian empire, then imagine that empire—too vast, weakening and falling apart, and
as a corollary, imagine the emancipation of its peoples: which
among them will gain supremacy and supply Europe with
that surfeit of impatience and power without which an irremediable stupor awaits her? I cannot doubt the answer:
it is those I have just mentioned. Given the reputation they
enjoy, my assertion will seem ludicrous. Central Europe,
just possibly . . . But the Balkans? —I don't want to defend
them, nor do I want to pass over their virtues in silence.
That taste for devastation, for internal clutter, for a universe
like a brothel on fire, that sardonic outlook on ancient or
imminent cataclysms, that pungency, that *far niente* of the
insomniac or the assassin—is it nothing, then, an inheritance
so rich and so burdensome, one that will thus empower
those who come into it? And who, stamped with a "soul,"
will thereby prove that they preserve a residue of savagery?
Insolent and despairing, they will choose to wallow in glory,
the appetite for which is inseparable from the will to self-
assertion and collapse, from the penchant for a *fast* twilight.
If their words are virulent, their accents inhuman and occasionally ignoble, this is because a thousand reasons impel
them to howl louder than civilized men who have exhausted
their cries. The last "primitives" in Europe, they may give
her a new energy, which she will not fail to regard as her
last humiliation. And yet, if the Balkans were no more than
horror, why is it, when we leave them and make for this
part of the world, why is it we feel a kind of fall—an admirable one, it is true—into the abyss?

Life in depth, the secret existence of peoples who, enjoying
the enormous advantage of having so far been rejected by

history, could capitalize their dreams—that buried existence doomed to the miseries of a resurrection begins on the other side of Vienna, a geographical extremity of Western decadence. Austria, whose erosion borders on the symbolic or the comical, prefigures Germany's fate. No sizable extravagance is left to the Germans, no further mission of frenzy, nothing to make them alluring or odious! Predestined barbarians, they destroyed the Roman Empire so that Europe could be born; having created it, they were appointed to destroy it; vacillating with them, Europe undergoes the recoil of their exhaustion. Whatever dynamism they still possess, they no longer have what underlies all energy, or what justifies it. Doomed to insignificance, budding Helvetians, forever banished from their habitual excess, reduced to brooding over their degraded virtues and their diminished vices, with, as their sole hope, the resource of being a mediocre tribe, the Germans are unworthy of the fear they still inspire: to believe in them or to be in dread of them is to do them an honor they scarcely deserve. Their failure was Russia's providence. Had they succeeded, she would have been sidetracked, for at least a century, from her great aims. But they could not succeed, for they attained to the peak of their material power at the very moment when they had nothing more to offer, when they were *strong* and empty. The hour had already struck for others. "Are not the Slavs the *ancient Germans*, with regard to the world which is disappearing?" asked Herzen in the middle of the last century—Herzen, the most perspicacious and lacerated of the Russian liberals, a mind of prophetic interrogations, disgusted by his own country, disappointed by the West, as unlikely to settle in a *patrie* as in a problem, though he loved to speculate on the life of peoples, a vague and inexhaustible subject, an émigré's pastime. Yet peoples, according to another Russian, Soloviev, are not what they imagine themselves to be, but what God thinks of them in His eternity. I have no information as to God's opinion of the Germans and the Slavs; nonetheless I know He has favored the latter, and that it is quite as futile to congratulate Him on the fact as to upbraid Him for it.

Today it is settled, that question so many Russians asked about their country in the last century: "Was this colossus created for nothing?" The colossus certainly has a meaning, and what a meaning! An ideological map would show that it extends beyond its borders, that it establishes its frontiers where it pleases, and that its presence evokes everywhere the notion less of a crisis than of an epidemic, salutary sometimes, frequently ruinous, always lightninglike.

The Roman Empire was the enterprise of a city; England's was established to remedy the exiguity of an island; Germany sought to build hers in order not to smother in an overpopulated territory. An unparalleled phenomenon, Russia was to justify her projected expansion in the name of her vast spaces. "The moment I have enough, why not have *too much*?" Such is the implicit paradox of both her proclamations and her silences. By converting infinity into a political category, she would overturn the classical concept and the traditional contexts of imperialism and provoke throughout the world a hope too great not to degenerate into chaos.

With her ten centuries of terrors, of shadows and promises, Russia was more likely than all others to adapt to the night side of our historical moment. Apocalypse suits her wonderfully, she has the habit of it, the taste for it, and functions within it today better than ever, since she has visibly changed rhythm. "Where are you rushing, O Russia?" Gogol already asked, perceiving the frenzy she concealed under her apparent immobility. We know where now, and above all we know that like all nations of an imperial destiny, she is more impatient to solve the problems of others than her own. Which is to say that our career *in time* depends on what she will decide or will undertake: she holds our future in her hands. . . . Fortunately for us, time does not exhaust our substance. The indestructible, the Elsewhere are conceivable: in us? apart from us? How can we tell? The fact remains that as things are now, only questions of strategy and metaphysics deserve our interest, those that rivet us to history and those that wrench us from it: actuality and the absolute, the newspapers and the Gospels. . . . I foresee the day when we shall read nothing but telegrams and prayers. A remarkable phenomenon: the more our immediacy absorbs us, the more we feel the need to offset it, so that we live, in one and the same moment, within the world and outside it. Hence, when we confront the sideshow of empires, all that remains for us to do is seek a middle term between the skull's grin and serenity.

Learning
from the Tyrants

===

Whoever has not known the temptation to be first in the city will understand nothing of how politics work, nothing of the passion to reduce others to the status of objects, and will never grasp the elements that constitute the art of contempt. Rare are those who have not suffered a thirst for power to some degree: it is natural to us, and yet, upon close consideration, it assumes all the characteristics of a morbid state from which we recover only accidentally or by some internal maturation, like the kind that occurred in Charles V when, abdicating at Brussels at the height of his glory, he taught the world that excessive lassitude could provoke scenes as admirable as excessive courage. But whether anomaly or marvel, renunciation, that challenge to our norms, to our identity, crops up only at exceptional moments, a limit-case that delights the philosopher and dumbfounds the historian.

Examine yourself when you are a prey to ambition, infected by its fever; then dissect your "fits." You will discover that they are preceded by strange symptoms, by a particular warmth which will not fail to overpower and alarm you. Future-sodden by abuse of hope, you suddenly feel responsible for now and what is to come, at the heart of a duration answerable to your every frisson and along with which—agent of a universal anarchy—you dream of exploding. Attentive to the events of your brain and the vicissitudes of your blood, brooding over your breakdown, you wait for its signs and cherish every one. Source of disorders, of peerless maladies, political mania, if it floods the intelligence, on the other hand favors the instincts and plunges you into a salutary chaos. The notion of the good and particularly of the evil you imagine you can accomplish will gladden and exalt you; and such will be the tour de force, the marvel of your infirmities, that they will set you up as master of everyone and everything.

Around you, you will notice an analogous breakdown in those eroded by the same passion. As long as they are under its spell, they will be unrecognizable, victims of an intoxication unlike any other. The very timbre of their voice, everything in them will change. Ambition is a drug that makes its addicts potential madmen. These stigmata, that lost-dog expression, those anxious features which seem to be twitching with a sordid ecstasy—if you haven't spotted them in yourself or in others, you will remain a stranger to the woes and wonders of Power, that tonic Hell, synthesis of poison and panacea.

Now imagine the converse process. The fever gone, lo! you are exorcised, normal *to excess*. No more ambition, hence no means of being someone or something; nothing personified, the void incarnate: glands and viscera clairvoyant, bones disabused, a body invaded by lucidity, pure of itself, out of the running and outside of time, hung upon a self fixed in a total knowledge without *acquaintances*. This moment vanished, where will you rediscover it—who will restore it to you? Everywhere men frenzied, men bewitched, a throng of deviants whom reason has deserted in order to take refuge in you, in the only one who has understood everything, absolute spectator lost among dupes, forever refractory to the unanimous farce. The interval which separates you from the rest incessantly widening, you come to wonder if you haven't perceived some reality hidden from everyone else. An infinitesimal or a crucial revelation, its content will remain obscure to you. The one thing you are sure of is your accession to a wholly new equilibrium, promotion of a mind free of all complicity with others. Unduly sane, more poised than all the sages, so you appear to yourself. . . . And if you still resemble the madmen around you, you feel that a trifle will distinguish you from them forever; imbued with this sensation or this illusion, even if you perform the same actions as other men, you do so without the same enthusiasm, the same conviction. Cheating will be for you a question of honor, and the only way of conquering your "fits" or of preventing their recurrence. If it has required nothing more or less than a revelation, or a collapse, you will deduce that those who have not suffered a crisis of this kind will sink ever deeper into the extravagances inherent in our race.

Have you noted the symmetry? In order to become a politician, that is, in order to have the stuff of a tyrant, a certain mental derangement is necessary; to cease being so, another derangement is no less in order: is it not a question, after all, of transforming our *folie des grandeurs?* To shift from wanting to be first in the city to wanting to be last, is, by a mutation of pride, to trade a dynamic madness for a static one, an extraordinary genre of insanity, as extraordinary as the renunciation which originates in it and which, answering to ascesis rather than to politics, has nothing to do with our subject.

For thousands of years, the appetite for power being dis-
persed in countless tyrannies, great and small, which have
raged here and there, the moment seems at hand when that
appetite must finally collect and concentrate in order to
culminate in a single power, expression of that thirst which
has devoured, which still devours the globe, last word of all
our dreams of mastery, the consummation of our hopes and
our aberrations. The scattered human herd will be united
under the guardianship of one pitiless shepherd, a kind of
planetary monster before whom the nations will prostrate
themselves in an alarm bordering on ecstasy. The universe
brought to its knees, an important chapter of history will
be closed. Then will begin the disintegration of this new
reign and the return to the primal disorder, to the old anarchy; the smothered hates and vices will reappear and with
them the minor tyrants of the bygone cycles. After the Great
Slavery, mediocre ones. But as they emerge from their monumental servitudes, the survivors will be proud of their
shame and of their fear and, incomparable victims, will cel-
ebrate its memory.

Dürer is my prophet. The more I observe the procession
of the centuries, the more I am convinced that the one image
capable of revealing its meaning is that of his *Four Horsemen
of the Apocalypse*. The ages advance only by treading the
hordes underfoot; the weak will die no less than the strong,
and even these riders, save *one*. It is for him, for his terrible
renown, that the ages have suffered and groaned. I see him
looming on the horizon, already I detect our whimpers, I
even hear our screams. And the night that will descend upon
our bones will not bring peace, as it did to the Psalmist, but
fear. Judging by the tyrants it has produced, our epoch will
have been anything but mediocre. To find their like, one

must go back to the Roman Empire or to the Mongol invasions. Even more than Stalin, it is Hitler who deserves the credit of having set our century's tone. He is important not so much in himself as in what he heralds, the rough draft of our future, harbinger of a grim advent and of a cosmic hysteria, precursor of that grand-scale despot who will succeed in unifying the world by science, destined not to deliver but to enslave us. This was understood long ago, it will be understood again one day. We are born to exist, not to know; to be, not to assert ourselves. Knowledge, having irritated and stimulated our appetite for power, will lead us inexorably to our ruin. It is Genesis, not our dreams and our systems, that has perceived our condition.

What we have learned by ourselves, whatever knowledge we have extracted from our own core, must be expiated by a further disequilibrium: fruit of an intimate chaos, of a specific or diffuse disease, of a disorder at the root of our existence, knowledge taints the economy of a human being. Each of us must pay for the slightest damage he inflicts upon a universe created for indifference and stagnation; sooner or later, he will regret not having left it intact. If this is true of knowledge, it is even truer of ambition, for to despoil others involves more serious and more immediate consequences than to despoil mystery, or simply matter. You begin by making others tremble, but others end by transmitting their terrors to you. This is why tyrants, too, live in fear. The fear our future master will know will doubtless be heightened by an ominous and unexampled felicity, appropriate to a solitary par excellence lording it over all humanity like a god enthroned in dread, in omnipotent panic without beginning or end, coupling the acrimony of a Prometheus with the impertinence of a Jehovah, a scandal for

the imagination and the mind, a provocation to mythology
and theology alike.

Once monsters have been billeted in a city, a kingdom,
or an empire, it is natural that more powerful ones should
appear, under cover of disaster, the liquidation of nations
and of our liberties. A context in which we achieve the
contrary of our aspirations, in which we disfigure them un-
ceasingly, History is certainly not of an angelic essence.
Upon considering it closely, we conceive only one desire:
to promote spleen to the dignity of a gnosis.

All men are more or less envious; politicians, envious
absolutely. A man becomes one of these only to the degree
that he endures no one beside or above himself. To venture
upon an undertaking of any kind, even the most insignificant, is to sacrifice to envy, supreme prerogative of the
living, law and resource of actions. When envy leaves you,
you are no more than an insect, a nothing, a shadow. And
a sick man. And if envy should sustain you, it assuages the
failures of pride, ministers to your interests, conquers apathy, and performs more than one miracle. Is it not strange
that no therapeutics, no ethics have recommended its benefits, whereas, more charitable than providence, envy pre-
cedes our steps in order to direct them? Woe to the man
who ignores, who neglects, or who shuns envy! Thereby he
shuns the consequences of original sin, the need to act, to
create, and to destroy. Incapable of envying others, what
would he seek among them? A derelict's destiny awaits him.
To be saved, he must be forced to model himself upon the
tyrants, to take advantage of their excesses and their misdeeds. It is from them, and not from the sages, that he will
learn how to enjoy things once more, how to live, how to
live down. Let him trace his way back toward sin, let him

reintegrate the Fall, if he too would share the general degradation, that euphoria of damnation in which all creatures are immersed. Will he then succeed? Nothing is less certain, for what he imitates of the tyrants is only their solitude. Pity him, then, pity a wretch who, not deigning to entertain his vices or to compete with others, falls short of himself and remains beneath all others.

If actions are fruits of envy, it will be understood why political struggle, in its ultimate expression, comes down to calculations and intrigues likely to assure the elimination of our rivals or our enemies. If you would strike home, begin by liquidating those who think according to your categories and your prejudices and, having traveled the same roads beside you, necessarily dream of supplanting or felling you. They are the most dangerous of your competitors; confine yourself to them, the others can wait. Were I to seize power, my first concern would be to do away with all my friends. Any other way of going about it would spoil the métier, would discredit tyranny. Hitler, quite competent in this instance, displayed great wisdom by getting rid of Roehm, the only man he addressed in the second person singular, and of a good number of his early companions. Stalin, for his part, was no less equal to the task, as the Moscow purges testify.

As long as a conqueror succeeds, as long as he gains ground, he can permit himself any atrocity; public opinion absolves him; once fortune abandons him, the slightest error turns against him. Everything depends on the *moment* when he kills: crime in full glory consolidates authority by the sacred fear it inspires. The art of making oneself feared and respected is equivalent to the sense of opportunity. Mussolini, the very type of the clumsy or unlucky despot, turned cruel when his failure was manifest and his prestige tarnished; a few months of inopportune vengeances voided the work of twenty years. Napoleon was much more perspicacious: had he had the Duke d'Enghien put to death later, after the Russian campaign for example, he would have bequeathed an image of himself as an executioner; instead, this murder now appears as a blot on his memory and nothing more.

If, at the limit, you can rule without crimes, you cannot do so without injustices. What counts is to determine the proper proportion of the former and the latter, and to commit both only by fits and starts. For them to be forgiven, they must appear to be the consequences of rage or madness, and the tyrant must give the impression of being bloodthirsty by inadvertence, pursuing hideous schemes under the mildest appearance. Absolute power is not a comfortable matter: only ham actors and assassins on a grand scale distinguish themselves in its possession. There is nothing more admirable humanly, and more lamentable historically, than a tyrant demoralized by his scruples.

"And the people?" it will be asked. The thinker or the historian who employs the word without irony disqualifies himself. It is all too clear what "the people" are destined for: to suffer events and rulers' whims, lending themselves to the schemes that weaken and overwhelm them. Every political experiment, however "advanced," is performed at the people's expense, is carried out against the people: the people bear the stigmata of slavery by divine or diabolic decree. No use wasting your pity: the people's cause admits of no recourse. Nations and empires are formed by the people's indulgence of iniquities of which they are the object. No head of state, no conqueror fails to scorn the people; but the people accept this scorn and live on it. Were they to cease being weak or victimized, were they to disappoint their destiny, society would collapse and with it history itself. Let us not be overoptimistic: nothing in the people permits us to envision such a splendid eventuality. As they are, the people represent an invitation to despotism. The people endure their ordeals, sometimes solicit them, and rebel against them only to rush into new ones, more horrible than the old. Revolution being their one luxury, they fling themselves into it, not so much to derive certain benefits from it or to improve their lot, as to acquire for themselves, too, the right to insolence, an advantage which consoles them for their habitual setbacks, but which they immediately lose once the privileges of chaos are abolished. Since no regime assures their salvation, the people adapt themselves to all and to none. And from the Flood to the Last Judgment, all they can claim is to fulfill their mission honestly: *to be vanquished.*

To return to our friends, beyond the reason invoked to get rid of them, there exists another: they know our limits and our defects too well (friendship comes down to this and nothing more) to entertain the slightest illusion as to our virtues. Hostile, moreover, to our promotion to the rank of idol (to which public opinion would be quite disposed), determined to safeguard our mediocrity, our *real* dimensions, they puncture the myth we would like to create in our behalf, they keep us at our exact measure, denounce the false image we have of ourselves. And when they grant us a little praise, they insinuate into it so many dark hints and subtleties that their flattery, by dint of circumspection, is equivalent to an affront. What they secretly long for is our collapse, our humiliation, and our ruin. Identifying our

success with a usurpation, they keep all their perspicacity
for the scrutiny of our thoughts and our actions in order to
expose their vanity, and show kindness only when we ourselves give evidence of decline. So lively is their enthusiasm
for the spectacle of our downfall that they really love us at
such times, sympathize with our miseries, avoid their own
in order to partake of ours and feast on them. During our
elevation, they observed us pitilessly, they were *objective*;
but now they can permit themselves the elegance of seeing
us as more than we are and of pardoning our former suc-
cesses, being convinced that we will enjoy no new ones.
And such is their penchant for us that they spend their best
hours pitying our deformities and gushing over our defects.
Caesar's great mistake was not to distrust his own people,
those who, observing him at close hand, could not warrant
his claim to divine lineage; they refused to deify him; the
mob consented to this, but the mob consents to everything.
Had he done away with his friends, Caesar, instead of an
ignoble death, would have enjoyed a prolonged apotheosis,
the superb deliquescence suited to a real god. For all his
sagacity, he had a certain naïveté—he did not realize that
our intimates are the worst enemies of our *statue*.

In a republic, that paradise of debility, the politician is a
petty tyrant who obeys the laws; but a strong personality
does not respect them, or rather respects only those he
creates. Expert in the unjustifiable, such a personality regards the *ultimatum* as the acme and honor of his career.
To be in a position to issue one, or several, certainly involves
the kind of pleasure in comparison to which the rest are
merely sham. I do not believe you can lay claim to the
command of affairs if you do not aspire to this unparalleled
provocation, the most insolent of all, even more execrable

than the aggression by which it is generally followed. "Of how many ultimatums is he guilty?" should be the question asked about a head of state. Is there none on his record? History disdains him, history which wakes up only in the horror chapters and is somnolent in those of tolerance, of liberalism, regimes in which temperaments wilt and in which the most virulent seem, at best, watered-down conspirators.

I pity those who have never conceived a dream of excessive domination, nor felt the times seething within themselves. In the days when Ahriman was my principle and my god, when I thirsted for barbarism, I brooded over the cavalcades within myself, hordes provoking one sweet catastrophe after the next! Foundered as I have, nowadays, in modesty, I nonetheless harbor a weakness for tyrants, whom I always prefer to redeemers and prophets; I prefer them because they do not take refuge in formulas; because their prestige is an equivocal one, their cravings self-destructive; whereas the others, possessed of a limitless ambition, disguise its aims under deceptive precepts, retreat from the citizen in order to rule over conscience, to occupy it, and, once implanted there, to create permanent ravages without incurring the reproach, however merited, of indiscretion or sadism. Compared to the power of a Buddha, a Jesus, or a Mohammed, what does that of the conquerors signify? Abandon the notion of glory unless you are tempted to found a religion! Though in this sector, most places are taken, and men do not resign them readily: the leaders of a sect, what are they if not founders of a religion to the second degree? From the point of view of effectiveness alone, a Calvin or a Luther, having launched conflicts still unresolved today, quite eclipses a Charles V or a Philip II. Spiritual Caesarism is more refined and richer in upheavals than Caesarism proper: if you would leave a name, attach it to a church rather than to an empire. You will thereby have neophytes enfeoffed to your fate or to your fads, followers you can save or mistreat as you like.

The leaders of a sect stop at nothing, for their very scruples constitute part of their tactics. But setting aside the sects, an extreme case, the mere desire to institute a religious order is worth more, in terms of ambition, than to rule a city or to conquer by force of arms. To insinuate yourself into men's minds, to become master of their secrets, to despoil them, in a sense, of themselves, of their uniqueness, to rob them even of the privilege, regarded as inviolable, of "conscience," what tyrant, what conqueror has aimed so high? Invariably the religious strategy will be subtler, and more suspect, than the political. Merely compare Loyola's *Spiritual Exercises*, so shrewd in their detached tone, with the barefaced policies of *The Prince*, and you will measure the distance separating the cunning of the confessional from that of a chancellery or a throne.

The more intense a spiritual leader's appetite for power, the more he is concerned—not without reason—to limit it in others. Who among us, left to himself, would not take up space, air itself, and regard himself as its owner? A society that seeks to be perfect should make the straitjacket fashionable or else obligatory. For man moves only to do evil. Religions, striving to cure him of his obsession with power and to give a nonpolitical direction to his aspirations, join the regimes of authority, since like them, though with other methods, they seek to dominate man, to humble his nature, his native megalomania. What consolidated their credit, what enabled them to triumph hitherto over our inclinations—I mean the ascetic element—is precisely what has ceased to gain a hold over us. A perilous liberation was to result; ungovernable in every sense, fully emancipated, released from our chains and our superstitions, we are ripe for the remedies of terror. He who aspires to total freedom achieves it only to return to his point of departure, to his initial servitude. Whence the vulnerability of developed societies, amorphous masses with neither idols nor ideals, dangerously lacking in fanaticism, devoid of organic links and so helpless amid their whims or their convulsions that they anticipate—and this is the sole dream of which they are still capable—the security and dogmas of the yoke. Unfit to assume any longer the responsibility for their destiny, they scheme, even more than primitive societies, for the advent of despotism, to be delivered from the last vestiges of an exhausted, drained, and futilely obsessive appetite for power.

A world without tyrants would be as boring as a zoo without hyenas. The master we await in terror will be precisely a connoisseur of corruption, in whose presence we shall all figure as carrion. Let him come, let him sniff us out, let him wallow in our exhalations! Already, a new odor hangs over the universe.

In order not to yield to political temptation, we must keep a close watch over ourselves at every moment. How to manage this, especially in a democratic regime, whose essential vice is to permit anyone at all to seek power and to give free rein to his ambitions? There results a pullulation of braggarts, of futureless quibblers, commonplace lunatics whom fatality refuses to *sign*, incapable of any true frenzy, inept at both triumph and collapse. Yet it is their very nullity that permits and secures our liberties, threatened as they are by exceptional personalities. A self-respecting republic should fall into a panic upon the appearance of a great man, should banish him from its midst, or at least forbid a legend to grow up around him. If a republic is reluctant to do such things, it is because, dazzled by its scourge, it no longer believes in its institutions or in its reasons for being. It is entangled in its laws, and these, which protect its enemy, dispose and commit the republic to failure. Succumbing to the excesses of its own tolerance, it spares the adversary that will not spare it in turn, authorizes the myths that erode and destroy it, letting itself be trapped in the suavities of its own executioner. Does a republic deserve to subsist when its very principles invite it to disappear? Tragic paradox of freedom: the mediocre men who alone make its exercise possible cannot guarantee its duration. We owe everything to their insignificance, and we lose everything by it. Thus they are always unequal to their task. It is this mediocrity that I hated in the days when I unreservedly loved the tyrants, of whom we can never say often enough that unlike their caricature (every democrat is an operetta tyrant), they have a destiny, even *too much* of one. And if I made them into a sort of cult, it was because, having the instinct of command, they do not lower themselves to dialogue or to arguments: they give orders, issue decrees, without condescending to justify their actions; whence their cynicism, which I set above all virtues and all vices, the sign of superiority, even of nobility, which, in my eyes, separated them from the rest of mortal men. Unable to render myself worthy of them by action, I hoped to do so by words, by the practice of sophism and enormity: to be as odious with the means of mind as they were with those of power, to devastate by language, to blow up the word and with it the world, to explode with one and the other, and finally to

collapse under their debris! Now, deceived by these extravagances, by all that once enlivened my days, I have come
to dream of a city, a marvel of moderation, ruled by a team
of slightly senile octogenarians, involuntarily amenable yet
still lucid enough to make good use of their decrepitudes,
exempt from desires, from regrets, from doubts, and so
concerned with the general equilibrium and the public welfare that they would regard even a smile as a sign of prof-
ligacy and of subversion. And such is at present my fallen
state that democrats themselves seem to me too ambitious,
too mad. I should still be their accomplice if their hatred
of tyranny were pure; but they abominate it only because
it relegates them to private life and confronts them with
their nothingness. The only order of greatness to which they
can attain is that of failure. Liquidation suits them well, they
are comfortable in it, and when they excel there, they deserve our respect. As a general rule, in order to lead a state
to ruin, there must be a certain ardor, particular tendencies,
even talents. But it may happen that circumstances are propitious; the task is then easy, as is proved by the example
of countries in decline, lacking inner resources, that fall prey
to the insoluble, to lacerations, to the play of contradictory
opinions and tendencies. Such was the case of ancient Greece.
With respect to failure, that of Greece was perfect: one
might say that she worked at it in order to offer it as a model
and to discourage posterity from making similar attempts.
Starting from the third century B.C., her substance wasted,
her idols wavering, her political life torn between the Mac-
edonian party and the Roman, Greece resorted—in order
to solve her crises, to remedy the curse of her liberties—
to foreign domination, and for over five hundred years ac-
cepted Rome's yoke, impelled to do so by the very degree

of refinement and gangrene to which she had attained. Once polytheism was reduced to a heap of fables, she would lose her religious and with it her political genius, two realities indissolubly linked: to call in question the gods is to call in question the city over which they preside. Greece could not survive them, any more than Rome would survive hers. That Greece lost, with her religious instinct, her political instinct, we are easily enough convinced by regarding her reactions during the civil war: always on the wrong side, joining Pompey against Caesar, Brutus against Octavius and Antony, Antony against Octavius, Greece regularly espoused misfortune, as if she had found in the continuity of fiasco a guarantee of stability, the solace and convenience of the irreparable. The more the evolved nations weary of their gods (and the gods themselves weary of them), the more readily they risk succumbing. The citizen is refined at the expense of institutions; no longer believing in them, he can no longer defend them. When the Romans, by contact with the Greeks, finally lost their vulgarity, that is, weakened, the days of the republic were numbered. The Romans resigned themselves to dictatorship, perhaps longed for it in secret: no Rubicon without the complicities of a collective fatigue.

The death principle inherent in all regimes is more perceptible in republics than in dictatorships: the former proclaim and parade it, the latter disguise and deny it. Nonetheless, despotisms, thanks to their methods, can ensure a longer and above all a more *comfortable* duration: they solicit, they cultivate events, while the others gladly forgo them, freedom being a state of absence, absence likely to . . . degenerate when citizens exhausted by the burden of being themselves aspire to nothing more than humiliation and defeat, thereby satisfying their nostalgia for servitude. Nothing more distressing than the exhaustion and the rout of a republic: it should be described in the tonality of elegy or epigram, or better still, in that of Montesquieu's *Spirit of the Laws*: "When Sulla sought to restore Rome her liberty, she could no longer receive it; she retained but a faint vestige of virtue; and, since she had continually less of this, instead of waking after Caesar, Tiberius, Caius, Claudius, Nero, Domitian, she was ever more enslaved: each blow fell upon the tyrant, none upon tyranny." This is so because tyranny is just what one can develop a taste for, since it so happens that man prefers to wallow in fear rather than to face the anguish of being himself. Generalize the phenomenon and the Caesars appear: how to blame them, when they answer the requirements of our misery and the pleas of our cowardice? They even deserve to be admired: they fling themselves upon assassination, constantly brood upon it, accept its horrors and its ignominy, and devote all their thoughts to it, to the point of forgetting suicide and exile, less spectacular formulas though gentler and more agreeable. Having opted for the most difficult, they can flourish only in uncertain times, sustaining chaos or else throttling it. The epoch favorable to their advance coincides with the end of a cycle of civilization. This is obvious with regard to the ancient world, and it will be no less so with regard to ours, which is heading straight for a much more considerable tyranny than the one rampant in the first centuries of our era. The most elementary meditation on the historical process of which we are the result reveals that Caesarism will be the mode by which the sacrifice of our liberties will be consummated. If the continents are to be welded together, unified, it is force that will do the job, not persuasion; like the Roman

Empire, the one to come will be forged by the sword and will be established with our unanimous collaboration, since our very terrors demand it.

If you accuse me of extravagance, I answer that it is indeed possible that I am anticipating somewhat hastily. The dates are of no importance. The first Christians expected the world to end from one minute to the next; they were off by merely a few thousand years. . . . In an entirely different order of expectation, I too may be mistaken; but finally, one neither tests nor proves a vision: mine of the coming tyranny strikes me as so decisively apparent that it seems unworthy to attempt to demonstrate its well-foundedness. It is a certitude that partakes of both the shudder and the axiom. To it I adhere with the passion of a convulsionary and the assurance of a geometrician. No, I am not extravagant, or mistaken. And I could not even say, with Keats, that the sentiment of shadows invades me. Rather it is a light that assails me, precise and intolerable, by which I envisage not the end of the world—that *would* be extravagant—but the end of a style of civilization and of a way of writing. To confine myself to what is at hand, and more particularly to Europe, it seems to me, with a final distinctness, that unity will not be formed, as some may suppose, by agreement and deliberation, but by violence, according to the laws that govern the construction of empires. For these old nations, steeped in their provincial obsessions, to renounce and be released from them will require a hand of iron, for they will never consent to such a thing of their own accord. Once enslaved, communing within humiliation and defeat, they can devote themselves to a supranational enterprise, under the vigilant and scornful eye of their new master. Their servitude will be brilliant, they will nurse it with eagerness and delicacy, lavishing indeed the last remains of their genius upon it. They will pay dearly for the luster of their slavery.

Thus Europe, ahead of time, will set, as always, an example to the world and win renown in her role as protagonist and as victim. Her mission consisted in prefiguring the ordeals of others, in suffering for them and before them, in offering them her own convulsions as a model, so that they would be dispensed from inventing original, personal ones. The more Europe exerted herself for them, the more she tormented herself in her struggles, the better they lived as parasites upon her pangs, as heirs of her revolutions. In the future too, they will turn to her, till the day when, spent, she can no longer bequeath them anything but her leavings.

Odyssey of Rancor

We spend the prime of our sleepless nights in mentally mangling our enemies, rending their entrails, wringing their veins, trampling each organ to mush, and charitably leaving them the skeleton to enjoy. Whereupon we forbear, overcome by fatigue, and drop off to sleep. A well-earned rest after so much scruple, so much zeal. Moreover we must recover our strength in order to begin all over again the next night—resuming a labor that would discourage the most Herculean butcher. No doubt about it: having enemies is no sinecure.

The program of our nights would be less crowded if by day we could give our resentment free rein. To achieve not even happiness, merely equilibrium, we need to liquidate a good number of our kind, to inflict a regular hecatomb in the fashion of our remote and relaxed ancestors. Not so relaxed, it will be objected—the caveman's demographic poverty denying him any continuous opportunity for slaughter. So be it! But he had compensations, he was better provided for than we are: rushing off to hunt at all hours, falling upon wild beasts, it was still his own species he was destroying. Blood-baptized, he could readily indulge his frenzy; no need for him to disguise and defer his sanguinary intentions, whereas we are doomed to review and repress our lust for rapine till it shrivels within us—reduced to curbing, to postponing, even to renouncing our revenge.

To forswear vengeance is to chain oneself to forgiveness, to founder in pardon, to be tainted by the hatred smothered within. . . . Spared, our enemy obsesses and aggrieves us, especially when we have *resolved* to abhor him no longer. Indeed we truly forgive him only if we have promoted or witnessed his fall, if he affords us the spectacle of an ig-nominious end or—supreme reconciliation!—if we contem-plate his corpse. Such happiness, in truth, is rare and not to be relied on. For our enemy is never felled: always erect, always triumphant, it is his nature to loom up before us, flouting our timid gibes by his full-blown scorn.

Nothing is more deleterious to happiness than the "duty" to resist our primal depths, to turn a deaf ear to the call of the wild. The result? Those torments of a civilized man reduced to smiling, harnessed to calumny, and disconsolate at having to kill without making a move—by the mere power of the Word, that invisible dagger. Various are the ways of cruelty. Supplanting the jungle, conversation permits our bestiality to function without immediate damage to our kind. If, by the whim of some malefic power, we should lose the use of speech, no one would survive unscathed. The need to kill, inscribed in every cell, we have managed to transfer to our thoughts: only this feat accounts for the possibility, and the permanence, of society. May we conclude that we have won out over our native corruption, our homicidal talents? That would be to miscalculate the Word's capacities and to exaggerate its powers. The cruelty which we have inherited, which we wield, is not to be so readily ruled; as long as we do not capitulate to it altogether, as long as we have not used it up, we preserve it in our secret self—we are never released from it. Your real murderer premeditates his deed, plans it out, performs it, and by doing so frees himself, for a time, from his impulses; on the other hand, the man who does not kill because he cannot, though he endures the craving to do so—the unrealized assassin, let us say, the elegiac trifler of carnage—mentally commits countless crimes, and suffers far worse for them, since he drags with him the regret for all the abominations he cannot perpetrate. In the same way, the man who shrinks from revenge poisons his days, curses both his scruples and that act *against nature*, pardon. Doubtless, revenge is not always sweet: once it is consummated, we feel *inferior* to our victim, or else we are tangled in the subtleties of remorse; so vengeance too has its venom, though it comes closer to what we are, to what we feel, to the very law of the self; it is also *healthier* than magnanimity. The Furies were held to antedate the gods, Zeus included. Vengeance before Divinity! This is the major intuition of ancient mythology.

Those who, whether from impotence, lack of opportunity, or grandstand generosity, have not reacted to their enemies' wiles, bear upon their faces the stigmata of repressed rage, the traces of affront and opprobrium, the dishonor of having forgiven. The blows they have not dealt are turned against themselves and collaborate, within their features, to illustrate their cowardice. Bewildered and obsessed, cornered by shame, saturated with bitterness, refractory to others as to themselves, as stifled as they are ready to explode, they seem to be making a superhuman effort to ward off a risk of convulsion. The greater their impatience, the more they must disguise it, and when they cannot, they give way at last, but to no purpose, stupidly, for it is in absurdity that they founder, like those who, having accumulated too much bile and too much silence, at the crucial moment lose all their powers before their enemies, of whom they show themselves to be unworthy. Their failure will further enhance their spite, and each experience, however trifling, will signify for them a further dose of gall.

We become good-natured, we become *good* only by destroying the best of our nature, only by submitting our body to the discipline of anemia and our mind to that of oblivion. As long as we preserve even a trace of memory, forgiveness comes down to a struggle with our instincts, an aggression against our own ego. It is our flagrancies that keep us in tune with ourselves, ensure our continuity, link us to our past, stimulate our powers of evocation; in the same way, our imaginations function only in hope of others' misfortune, in the raptures of disgust, in that disposition which impels us if not to commit infamies, at least to contemplate them. How could it be otherwise on a planet where flesh propagates with the shamelessness of a scourge? Wherever we go, we come up against the human, a repulsive ubiquity before which we fall into stupor and revolt, a perplexity *on fire*. Once, when space was less crowded, less infested by mankind, certain sects, indubitably inspired by a beneficent power, advocated and practiced castration; by an infernal paradox, they have been suppressed just when their doctrine would have been more opportune and more salutary than ever before. Maniacs of procreation, bipeds with devalued faces, we have lost all appeal for each other. And it is only on a half-deserted earth, peopled at most by a few thousand inhabitants, that our physiognomies might recover their ancient glamour. The multiplication of our kind borders on the obscene; the duty to love them, on the preposterous.

Which does not keep our thoughts from being contaminated by the presence of the human, from *stinking* of the human, and from being unable to cleanse themselves of it. Of what truths are we capable, to what revelation can we rise, when this pestilence asphyxiates the mind and disqualifies it from considering anything but the pernicious and fetid animal whose emanations it endures? He who is too weak to declare war on mankind must never forget, in his moments of fervor, to pray for a second Flood, more radical than the first.

Knowledge subverts love: in proportion as we penetrate our own secrets, we come to loathe our kind, precisely because they resemble us. When we have no further illusions about ourselves, we retain none about others; the unspeakable that we discover by introspection we extend, by a legitimate generalization, to other mortals; depraved in their essence, we rightly endow them with all the vices which, oddly enough, most of us turn out to be unfit for or averse to ferreting out, to observing in ourselves or in others. How easy it is to do evil: everyone manages; but to *assume* it explicitly, to acknowledge its inexorable reality, is an unwonted feat. In practice, anyone can compete with the devil; in theory, this is not the case. To commit horrors and to conceive *horror* are two irreducible actions: no common ground between the experience of cynicism and cynicism in the abstract. Let us beware of those who subscribe to a reassuring philosophy, who believe in the Good and willingly erect it into an idol; they could not have done so if, honestly peering into themselves, they had sounded their depths or their miasmas; but those—rare, it is true—who have been indiscreet or unfortunate enough to plunge all the way down to the bottom of their beings, they know how to judge man: they can no longer love him, for they no longer love themselves, though remaining—and this will be their punishment—nailed even faster to themselves than before. . . .

In order to keep the faith, our own and others', in order to lose sight of the illusory character, the nullity of all action, nature has made us opaque to ourselves, subject to a blindness which generates and rules the world. Were we to undertake an exhaustive self-scrutiny, disgust would paralyze us, we would be doomed to a thankless existence. The incompatibility between action and self-knowledge seems to have escaped Socrates; otherwise, in his capacity as pedagogue, as man's ally, would he have dared adopt the oracle's motto, with all the abysses of renunciation it implies?

As long as we possess a will of our own, and as long as we are bound to it (this is what Lucifer has been blamed for), revenge is an imperative, an organic necessity which defines the universe of diversity, of the "self," and which can have no meaning in the universe of identity. If it were true that "we breathe in the One" (Plotinus), on whom would we take revenge where every difference is blurred, where we commune in the indiscernible and lose our contours there? As a matter of fact, we breathe in the multiple; our kingdom is that of the "I," and through the "I" there is no salvation. To exist is to condescend to sensation, hence to self-affirmation; whence not-knowing (with its direct consequence: revenge), the principle of phantasmagoria, source of our peregrination on earth. The more we try to wrest ourselves from our ego, the deeper we sink into it. Try as we will to explode it, just when we suppose we have succeeded, there it is, apparently more self-assured than ever; whatever we do to destroy it merely augments its strength and solidity, and such is its vigor and its perversity that it

flourishes still more in affliction than in joy. As with the
ego, so a fortiori with actions. When we imagine ourselves
liberated from them, we are anchored in them more fixedly
than ever: even when corrupted into simulacra, actions prevail over us, subject us to themselves. Whether an enterprise
is undertaken reluctantly or by persuasion, we always end
by adhering to it, becoming its slaves or its dupes. No man
stirs without allying himself to the multiple, to appearances,
to the "I." To act is to forfeit the absolute.

Action's sovereignty comes, let us admit it straight off,
from our vices, which master a greater contingent of existence than our virtues possess. If we espouse the cause of
life and more particularly that of history, they seem useful
to the supreme degree: is it not thanks to our vices that we
cling to things, and that we cut something of a figure here
on earth? Inseparable from our condition, vices are ubiq-
uitous: only the puppet is without them. To try to boycott
them is to conspire against ourselves, to lay down our arms
in the midst of battle, to discredit ourselves in our neighbor's
eyes or to remain forever void. The miser deserves to be
envied not for his money but precisely for his avarice, his
real treasure. By attaching the individual to a sector of reality, implanting him there, vices, which do nothing lightly,
occupy him, intensify him, justify his alienation from the
vague. The practical value of manias, of derangements and
aberrations, is irrefutable: insofar as we limit ourselves to
this world, to the here and now where our desires confront
one another, where competitiveness is rampant, even a minor
vice is more effective than a major virtue. The *political* dimension of beings (taking the political as the fulfillment of
the biological) safeguards the realm of actions, the realm of
dynamic abjection. To know ourselves is to identify the

sordid motive of our gestures, the inadmissible that is inscribed within our substance, the totality of patent or clan-
destine miseries on which our welfare depends. Whatever
emanates from the inferior zones of our nature is invested
with strength, whatever comes from below stimulates: we
invariably produce and perform better out of jealousy and
greed than out of nobility and disinterestedness. Sterility
awaits those who do not deign to encourage or divulge their
flaws. Whatever the domain to which we owe allegiance, in
order to excel there we must cultivate the insatiable aspect
of our character, must urge our inclinations to fanaticism,
to intolerance, to vindictiveness. Nothing is more suspect
than fruitfulness. If purity is what you seek, if you aspire
to some inner transparency, make haste to abdicate your
talents, abandon the realm of actions, exile yourself from
the human, renounce—to use the pious jargon—the "conversation of creatures."

Great gifts, far from excluding great defects, actually stip-
ulate and reinforce them. When the saints accuse themselves
of this or that sin, we must take them at their word. The
very interest they take in others' suffering testifies against
them. Their pity, pity in general—what is pity but the *vice*
of kindness? Deriving its effectiveness from the wicked
principle it conceals, pity delights in others' ordeals, postulates hell as a promised land it cannot do without, and if
it is not destructive in and of itself, nonetheless profits by
all that destroys. Extreme aberration of kindness, pity ends
up as its own negation, in the saints even more than among
ourselves. To be convinced of this, merely frequent their
lives and contemplate the voracity with which they fling
themselves upon our sins, their nostalgia for illustrious disgrace or interminable remorse, their exasperation before

the mediocrity of our misdeeds and their regret at not having to torment themselves more deeply for our redemption.

High as one mounts, one remains a captive of one's nature, of one's original debacle. Men of great ambitions, or simply of talents, are monsters, superb and hideous monsters who seem to be plotting some terrible crime; and in truth, they are preparing their work . . . creating it in secret, like criminals: must they not crush all those who would take the same path as themselves? A man strives and creates only to crush beings or Being, rivals or the Rival. At every level, minds war upon each other, delight and wallow in defiance: the saints themselves envy and exclude one another—like the gods, moreover: witness those perpetual scuffles which are the scourge of every Olympus. Anyone approaching the same domain or the same problem as ourselves jeopardizes our originality, our privileges, the integrity of our existence, strips us of our chimeras and our chances. The task of casting him down, of defeating or at least disparaging him assumes the form of a mission, even of a fatality. We are satisfied only by someone who abstains, who in no way manifests himself, yet he must also not accede to the rank of *model*: the *acknowledged* sage excites and legitimates our envy. Even an idler, if he distinguishes himself in his sloth, if he *shines* there, risks being reviled: he attracts too much attention to himself. . . . The ideal would be a well-proportioned effacement. No one has managed that.

We acquire glory only to the detriment of others, of those who seek it too, and there is no reputation that is not won at the cost of countless abuses. The man who has emerged from anonymity, or who merely strives to do so, proves that he has eliminated every scruple from his life, that he has triumphed over his conscience, if by some chance he ever had such a thing. To renounce one's name is to be doomed to inactivity; to cling to it is to degrade oneself. Must we either pray or write prayers? exist or express ourselves? One thing is sure: the principle of expansion, immanent in our nature, makes us regard others' merits as an encroachment upon our own, a continual provocation. If glory is forbidden, or inaccessible, we blame those who have attained it: they could have done so, we believe, only by keeping us from it; it was ours by right, belonged to us, and without the machinations of these usurpers, it would have been ours. "Much more than property, it is glory which is theft"— motto of the embittered and, to a degree, of us all. The delights of being unknown or misunderstood are rare; yet upon consideration, are they not equivalent to the pride of having triumphed over honors and vanities? to the desire for an unwonted renown, for fame *without a public?* Which is certainly the supreme form, the *summum* of the appetite for glory.

Nor is the word too strong: it is indeed an *appetite* which thrusts its roots into our senses and which answers to a physiological necessity, to a cry of our vitals. In order to forsake it, in order to conquer it, we should have to meditate upon our insignificance, assent to it fully yet derive no pleasure from doing so, for our certainty of being nothing leads, if we are not careful, to complacency and pride: we do not perceive our own nothingness, or linger over it for long, without clinging to it . . . sensually. A certain happiness enters into our lust to denounce the fragility of happiness; and in the same way, when we profess to scorn glory we are far from being unfamiliar with the thirst for it, we sacrifice to glory just when we proclaim its inanity. A loathsome desire, certainly, but inherent in our organization; in order to extirpate it, we must condemn flesh and spirit alike to petrifaction, must compete with the mineral kingdom in unconcern, then forget the others, evacuate them from our consciousness, for the mere fact of their presence, radiant and fulfilled, wakens our evil genius who commands us to sweep them away and to forsake our obscurity in order to eclipse their brilliance.

We resent everyone who has "chosen" to live in the same epoch as ourselves, those who run at our side, who hamper our stride or leave us behind. In clearer terms: all contemporaries are odious. We resign ourselves to the superiority of a dead man, never to that of the living, whose very existence constitutes a reproach and a censure, an invitation to the intoxications of modesty. That so many of our kind surpass us is as obvious as it is intolerable, and to be evaded by arrogating to ourselves the advantage of being unique. We gasp for breath among our competitors or our models: what a comfort to be among their tombs! The disciple himself breathes freely and enjoys his freedom only upon the master's death. All of us, insofar as we exist, pray for the downfall of those who eclipse us by their gifts, their labors, or their feats, and with greed, feverish greed, we await their last moments. Suppose this one climbs, in our own realm, above us; reason enough for us to want to be rid of him: how to forgive him the admiration he inspires, the secret and vexatious worship we shower upon him? Let him be gone, let him fade away, let him be done with, in fact, be dead, if we are to revere him without laceration, without acrimony, if our martyrdom is to cease!

With any brains at all, instead of thanking us for our propensity, he would hold it against us, would tax us with imposture, reject us with disgust or commiseration. Too full of himself, with no experience of the calvary of admiration, or of the contradictory impulses it provokes in us, he never suspects that by putting him on a pedestal we have consented to demean ourselves, and that this humiliation will have to be paid for—by him: could we ever forget what a blow— unwittingly, we grant him *that*—he has dealt to the sweet illusion of our singularity and our value? Having committed the imprudence, or the abuse, of letting himself be adored too long, now he must suffer the consequences: by the decree of our lassitude, he turns from a real god to a false one, reduced to a regret that he took up so much of our time. Perhaps we venerated him only in hopes of someday taking our revenge. If we love to prostrate ourselves, we love still more to deny those before whom we have groveled. Every undermining labor exalts, confers energy; whence the urgency, whence the practical infallibility of vile sentiments. Envy, which makes a fool into a daredevil, a worm into a tiger, whips up our nerves, ignites our blood, communicates to the body a shudder that keeps it from going soft, lends the most anodyne countenance an expression of concentrated ardor; without envy, there would be no events, nor even a *world*; indeed it is envy that has made man possible, permitted him to gain a name for himself, to accede to greatness *by the fall*, by that rebellion against the anonymous glory of paradise, to which—any more than the Fallen Angel, his inspiration and his model—he could not adapt himself. Everything that breathes and moves testifies to the initial taint. Forever associated with the effervescences of Satan (patron of Time, scarcely distinct from God, being merely His *visible* countenance), we are victims of this genius of sedition who persuades us to perform our task as living men by rousing us against one another in a deplorable combat, no doubt, but a fortifying one: we emerge from torpor, enlivened whenever—triumphing over our Higher Impulses—we become aware of our role as destroyers.

Admiration, on the contrary, by eroding our substance, depresses and ultimately demoralizes us; hence we turn against the *admired*—anyone guilty of having inflicted upon us the task of raising ourselves to his level. He must not be surprised if our ascent toward him is followed by backsliding, or if we sometimes revise our enthusiasms. It is our instinct for self-preservation that reminds us of our duty to ourselves, that compels such reassessments. We do not cease to esteem or to extol someone because his merits are in question, but because we can enhance ourselves only at his expense. Without being exhausted, our capacity for admiration suffers a crisis during which, given over to the pleasures and paroxysms of apostasy, we enlist our idols in order to repudiate and smash them one after the other, and this iconoclastic frenzy, shameful in itself, is nonetheless the force that vivifies our faculties.

A vulgar, hence effective, goad to inspiration, resentment triumphs in art, which cannot do without it—any more than philosophy, moreover: to think is to take a cunning revenge, in which we camouflage our baseness and conceal our lower instincts. Judged by what it excludes and rejects, a system suggests a settling of accounts, skillfully executed. Philosophers, like poets, like everyone who has something to say, are pitiless. If the gentle and the tepid leave no trace, it is not for lack of perspicacity or of depth, but of aggression, which nonetheless implies no integral vitality. At grips with the world, the thinker is often a weakling, a rachitic runt, all the more virulent for realizing his own biological inferiority and suffering from it. The more he is rejected by life, the more he tries to master it, to subjugate it, though unable to do so. Sufficiently disinherited to pursue happiness, yet too proud to find it or to resign himself to it, at once real and unreal, formidable and impotent, the thinker suggests a synthesis of beast and ghost, a madman who lives by metaphor.

An abiding, vigilant rancor can constitute, all by itself, the armature of an individual: weakness of character proceeds in most cases from a poor memory. Not to forget an insult is one of the secrets of success, an art invariably possessed by men with strong convictions, for every conviction consists chiefly of hate, and only secondly of love. Perplexities, on the other hand, are the lot of the man who, equally inept at hating or loving, has nothing to choose, not even his lacerations. If he would assert himself, shake off his apathy, play a part, let him invent enemies and cling to them, let him waken his dormant cruelty or the memory of outrages imprudently despised! To take the smallest step forward, even just to exist, requires a minimum of villainy. Let no one abandon his holdings in indignity if he wants to "persevere in being." Rancor preserves; if, moreover, we can sustain it, nurture it, we avoid softness and insipidity. We should even encourage it toward *things*: what better tactic for arming ourselves against them, for lowering ourselves advantageously to reality? A pure sentiment, lacking any vital charge, is a contradiction in terms, an impossibility, a fiction. Indeed there is no such thing, even if we sought it in religion, a realm where it is supposed to flourish. We do not undertake to exist, still less to pray, without sacrificing to the devil. In most cases we attach ourselves to God in order to take revenge on life, to punish it, to signify we can do without it, that we have found something better; and we also attach ourselves to God in horror of men, in reprisal against them, to make them understand that, having entrée elsewhere, we do not find their society indispensable, and that if we grovel before Him, it is in order not to have to grovel before them. Without this shabby, murky, secret element, our fervor would lack energy—perhaps it could not even exist.

The unreality of pure sentiments—we might suppose that it was the sick who could best reveal such a thing to us, that this was their mission and the meaning of their ordeals. Nothing more natural, since it is in the sick that the flaws of our race are concentrated and exacerbated. Having ranged through the various species, having striven with more or less success to imprint its sign upon them, Disease, weary of its progress, doubtless longed for rest and sought someone over whom to declare its supremacy in peace, someone who would prove quite amenable to its whims and its despotism, someone on whom it could really count. Experimenting left and right, Disease suffered many a failure, until at last it found man—unless it created him. Thus we are all sick men, some potentially so—the mass of the healthy, the type of placid, harmless humanity—the others actual, the diseased strictly speaking, a cynical and impassioned minority. Two categories close in appearance, irreconcilable in fact: a considerable gap separates possible pain from the real thing.

Instead of turning against ourselves, against the fragility of our complexion, we make others responsible for our condition, for the slightest discomfort, even for a headache, we accuse them of making us pay for their health, of being nailed to our sickbed so that they can move about as they choose. With what pleasure would we not see our disease, or our discomfort, spread, gain a following, and if possible extend to all humanity! Disappointed in our hopes, we resent everyone, near or far, we harbor *exterminating* sentiments, we want others to be even more seriously threatened than ourselves—let the hour of final agony, of a splendid mutual annihilation, toll for all the living! Only great sufferings, *unforgettable* sufferings, detach us from the world; the others, average pains, morally the worst kind, enslave us to it because they stir up the soul's lower depths. We must be on guard against the sick, they have "character" and can exploit and sharpen their rancors. One day, one of their number decided never again to shake hands with a well person; he soon discovered that many of those he had suspected of health were at bottom unscathed by it. Then why should he make enemies for himself on hasty suspicions? From all evidence, this man was more reasonable than the rest, and had scruples not habitual to the breed he belonged to, a frustrated, insatiable, and prophetic gang which ought to be isolated because it seeks to overturn the world in order to impose its law. Instead, let us put matters in the hands of the normal, the only ones disposed to leave things as they are: indifferent to both past and future, they confine themselves to the present, installing themselves there without hopes and without regrets. But as soon as health wavers, a man dreams of nothing but paradise and inferno, that is, he *reforms*: he seeks to amend the irreparable, to redress or demolish society, which he can no longer endure because he can no longer endure himself. A man who suffers is a public menace, a disequilibrated being, all the more fearsome in that he usually has to conceal his pain, the source of his energy. We cannot assert ourselves, or play a role here on earth, without help from some infirmity, and there is no dynamism that is not the sign of physiological misery or internal devastation. When we know equilibrium we care for nothing, we do not even feel attached to life, for we *are* life; once equilibrium is destroyed, instead of identifying ourselves with things, we think of nothing but overthrowing or molding them. Pride emanates from the tension and the strain of consciousness, from the impossibility of existing naïvely. Now the sick, never naïve, substitute for the given a false idea of it that they create, so that their perceptions and even their reflexes participate in a system of obsessions so imperious they cannot help codifying and inflicting them on others, perfidious legislators concerned to make their pains obligatory, in order to strike down those resolved not to share them. If the healthy seem more accommodating, if they have no reason to be intractable, it is because they are unaware of the explosive virtues of humiliation. He who has suffered humiliation will never forget its effects and will know no rest until he has put them into a work capable of perpetuating its pangs. To create is to bequeath one's sufferings, wanting others to enter into them, to assume them, to be impregnated by them, and to live them over again. This is true of a poem, this can be true of the cosmos. Without the hypothesis of a feverish deity subject to convulsions, giddy with epilepsy, we could not explain a universe that everywhere shows signs of an original sputum. . . . And we divine the essence of such a God only when we ourselves suffer fits such as He must have known at the moments He came to grips with Chaos. We are reminded of Him by everything in ourselves that resists form or good sense, by our confusions and our delirium: we join Him by supplications in which we dislocate ourselves in

Him and Him in us, for He is close to us whenever something in ourselves breaks down and when, in our fashion, we too measure ourselves against Chaos. A summary theology? Contemplating this botched Creation, how can we help incriminating its Author, how—above all—suppose Him able and adroit? Any other God would have given evidence of more competence or more equilibrium than this one: errors and confusion wherever you look! Impossible to absolve Him, but impossible, too, not to understand Him. And we understand Him by everything in ourselves that is fragmentary, incomplete, and inopportune. His enterprise bears the stigmata of the provisional, yet it is not time He lacked in order to finish things off. He was, to our misfortune, inexplicably rushed. By a legitimate ingratitude, and to make Him feel the brunt of our ill humor, we set about—experts in counter-Creation—deteriorating His structure, rendering even messier a work already compromised from the start. Doubtless it would be wiser and more elegant to have nothing to do with it, to leave it as it is, not to exact reprisal for His own incapacities; but since He has transmitted His defects to us, we cannot show Him much solicitude. If, all things considered, we prefer Him to humanity, this does not exempt Him from our resentment. Perhaps we have conceived Him only to justify and regenerate our rebellions, to afford them a worthy object, to keep them from spoiling and dwindling, reinforcing them by the inspiriting abuse of sacrilege, an answer to the arguments and seductions of discouragement. We are never quite finished with God. Treating Him on equal footing as an enemy is an impertinence that fortifies, stimulates, and how much we must pity those He has ceased to annoy. What luck, on the other hand, to be able without embarrassment to make

Him assume responsibility for all our miseries, to overwhelm and insult Him, to spare Him nothing at any moment,
not even in our prayers!

To rancor, on which we have no monopoly, He too is
subject (as many a Sacred Book attests), for solitude, however absolute, is no defense against it. That even for God
it is not good to be alone signifies, in short: let Us create
the world to have something to get back at, on which to
practice Our verve and Our victimization. And when the
world goes up in smoke, there remains, whether one is man
or God, this subtle form of vengeance: vengeance against
oneself, an absorbing occupation, anything but destructive
since it proves that one still makes terms with life, that one
adheres to it precisely by the tortures one inflicts upon
oneself. Hosanna is not one of our habits. Equally impure,
though in different ways, divine and diabolic principles are
easy to conceive of; angels, on the contrary, exceed our
grasp. And if we cannot quite envision them, if they fluster
our imagination, it is because, unlike God, the devil, and
all the rest of us, angels alone—when they are not the Exterminating variety!—thrive without the spur of rancor. And—
need we add?—without that of flattery, which busy animals
like ourselves cannot do without. We depend, in order to
create, upon the opinion of our neighbors, we solicit, we
implore their homage, we mercilessly pursue those among
them who offer us nuanced or even equitable judgments,
and if we had the means, we should oblige them to bear
exaggerated, ridiculous ones, out of all proportion to our
aptitudes or our accomplishments. All measured praise being
identified with injustice, objectivity with provocation, reserve with insult, what keeps the universe from flinging itself
at our feet? What we crave, what we want to see in others'

eyes, is that servile expression, an unconcealed infatuation with our gestures and our lucubrations, the avowal of an ardor without second thoughts, an ecstasy before our nothingness. A profiteering moralist—a psychologist paired with a parasite—the flatterer knows our weakness and shamelessly exploits it. So far have we fallen that we accept all excesses, premeditated and false claims of admiration, at face value, without a blush, for we prefer the enthusiasms of mendacity to the indictment of silence. Commingled with our physiology, our viscera, flattery affects our glands, stimulates our secretions, and seeks out, moreover, our basest feelings, hence our most profound and natural ones, provoking in us a second-rate euphoria to which we give our flabbergasted attention; quite as flabbergasted, we contemplate the even more marked effects of censure, which invade and overwhelm the very depths of our being. Since no one rebukes us with impunity, we reply either by immediately striking back or by generating gall, the equivalent of a seasoned riposte. *Not* to react would require a metamorphosis, a total transformation not only of our dispositions, but of our organs themselves. Such an operation not being imminent, we bow with good grace to the maneuvers of flattery and the sovereignty of rancor.

To repress the need for revenge is to try to dismiss time, to deny events the possibility of occurring—it is to seek to get rid of evil and, with it, of action. But action, a hunger for defeat consubstantial with the self, is a fury over which we triumph only at those moments when, weary of tormenting our enemies, we abandon them to their fate, leaving them to rot because we do not *love* them enough to bother to destroy them, to dissect them, to make them the object of our nocturnal anatomies. Yet the frenzy comes upon us again, once that lust for appearances revives, that passion for the absurd which constitutes our passion for existence. Even reduced to the infinitesimal, life feeds on itself, tends toward an increase of being, seeks to grow for no reason, by a dishonoring and irrepressible automatism. One and the same thirst devours gnat and elephant; with any luck it might have been vanquished in humanity; we have seen that this was not the case: the craving breaks out everywhere, with increased intensity among the bedridden themselves. Capacity for *desistance* constitutes the sole criterion of spiritual progress: it is not when things leave us, it is when we leave them that we accede to an inner nakedness, to that extremity where we no longer affiliate ourselves with this world or with ourselves, and where victory signifies resignation, serene self-renunciation without regrets and above all without melancholy; for melancholy, discreet and aerial as it may appear, still derives from resentment: it is a reverie stamped with harshness, a jealousy disguised as languor, a vaporous rancor, but rancor. As long as we remain in its power, we desist from nothing, we are bogged down in the "I," yet without release from others, whom we think of all the more obsessively if we have not managed to prise ourselves loose from . . . ourselves. At the very moment we promise ourselves to vanquish vengeance, we feel it stirring within us more powerfully than ever, ready to take the offensive. "Forgiven" transgressions suddenly demand reparation, invade our sleepless nights and, even more, our dreams, turning them into nightmares, venturing so deep into our abysses that they end by forming their very substance. If this be so, what is the use of acting out the farce of noble sentiments, gambling on a metaphysical risk, or anticipating redemption? To take revenge, even if only in thought, is irremediably to place ourselves on this side of the absolute. Absolute indeed! Not only insults "forgotten" or silently endured, but even those we have repaid, harass and haunt us to the end of our days, and this obsession which should disqualify us in our own eyes actually succors us, makes us eager for battle. The slightest affront, a word, a glance tainted by some restriction—these we never pardon a living person. Nor do we even pardon such things after that person's death. The image of his corpse doubtless assuages us and compels us to indulgence; once the image blurs and in our memory the face of the living man prevails over and replaces that of the deceased, our old rancors rise up again, resume all the more powerfully, with that whole procession of shames and humiliations which will last as long as ourselves and whose memory would be eternal, had immortality devolved upon us.

Since everything wounds and insults us, why not swathe ourselves in skepticism and try to find a remedy for our distress? This would be only another deception, since Doubt is merely a product of our irritations and our grievances— the instrument a flayed man uses to suffer and to cause suffering. If we demolish certainties, it is from no theoretical scruple or in a playful spirit, but out of a craving to see them vanish—also out of a desire that they belong to no one, once they desert us and we possess none. And the truth? By what right would others have access to the truth? By what injustice would it be revealed to them, who are worth less than ourselves? Have they striven, have they lain awake to deserve it? While we labor in vain to attain truth, they strut about as if it were set apart for them, as if they were endowed with it by some providential decree. Yet truth cannot be their appanage, and to keep them from laying claim to it, we convince them that when they imagine they possess it, it is actually a fiction that they grasp. In order to salve our own consciences, we delight in labeling their bliss nothing but ostentation and arrogance, which allows us to disturb them without remorse and, by inoculating them with our stupors, to make them as vulnerable and wretched as ourselves. Skepticism is the sadism of embittered souls.

The more stress we lay on our torments, the more inseparable they seem from our unredeemed condition. The maximum detachment to which we can lay claim is a position equidistant from vengeance and from pardon, halfway between a resentment and a generosity equally limp and spent, since destined to neutralize one another. But to slough off the old Adam—that we shall never manage, even if we were to carry horror of ourselves to the point of forever renouncing any rank at all in the hierarchy of beings.

Mechanism of Utopia

Whenever I happen to be in a city of any size, I marvel that riots do not break out every day: massacres, unspeakable carnage, a doomsday chaos. How can so many human beings coexist in a space so confined without destroying each other, without hating each other *to death*? As a matter of fact, they do hate each other, but they are not equal to their hatred. And it is this mediocrity, this impotence, that saves society, that assures its continuance, its stability. Occasionally some shock occurs by which our instincts profit; but afterward we go on looking each other in the face as if nothing had happened, cohabiting without too obviously tearing each other to shreds. Order is restored, a ferocious calm as dreadful, ultimately, as the frenzy that had interrupted it.

Yet I marvel still more that some of us, society being what it is, have ventured to conceive another one altogether—a different society. What can be the cause of so much naïveté, or of so much inanity? If the question is normal enough, even ordinary, the curiosity that led me to ask it, on the other hand, has the excuse of being morbid.

Seeking new evidence, and just as I despaired of finding anything of the kind, it occurred to me to consult utopian literature, to steep myself in its "masterpieces," to *wallow* in them. There, to my great delight, I sated my pentitential longings, my appetite for mortification. To spend months recording the dreams of a better future, of an "ideal" society, devouring the unreadable—what a windfall! I hasten to add that this tedious literature has much to teach, and that time spent frequenting it is not entirely wasted. From the start, one discerns in it the (fruitful or calamitous) role taken, in the genesis of events, not by happiness but by the *idea* of happiness, an idea that explains—the Age of Iron being coextensive with history—why each epoch so eagerly invokes the Age of Gold. Suppose we put an end to such speculations: total stagnation would ensue. For we *act* only under the fascination of the impossible: which is to say that a society incapable of generating—and of dedicating itself to—a utopia is threatened with sclerosis and collapse. Wisdom—fascinated by nothing—recommends an existing, a *given* happiness, which man rejects, and by this very rejection becomes a historical animal, that is, a devotee of *imagined* happiness.

"A new heaven and a new earth: for the first heaven and the first earth were passed away," we read in Revelations. Cross out "heaven," just keep the "new earth," and you have the secret and the recipe of all utopian systems; for greater precision, perhaps you should put "city" for "earth"; but that is only a detail; what counts is the prospect of a new advent, the fever of an essential expectation—a debased, modernized Parousia from which arise those systems so dear to the disinherited. Poverty is in fact the utopianist's great auxiliary, it is the matter he works in, the substance on which he feeds his thoughts, the providence of his obsessions. Without poverty he would be empty; but poverty occupies him, allures or embarrasses him, depending on whether he is poor or rich; from another point of view, poverty cannot do without him—it needs this theoretician, this adept of the future, especially since poverty itself, that endless meditation on the likelihood of escaping its own present, would hardly endure its dreariness without the obsession of *another* earth. Can you doubt it? If so, it is because you have not tasted utter indigence. Do so and you will see that the more destitute you are, the more time and energy you will spend in reforming everything, in thinking—in other words, in vain. I have in mind not only institutions, human creations: those of course you will condemn straight off and without appeal; but objects, all objects, however insignificant. Unable to accept them as they are, you will want to impose your laws and your whims upon them, to function at their expense as legislator or as tyrant; you will even want to intervene in the life of elements in order to modify their physiognomy, their structure. Air annoys you: let it be transformed! And stone as well. And the same for the vegetal world, the same for man. Down past the foundations of being, down to the strata of chaos, descend, install yourself there! When you haven't a penny in your pocket, you strive, you dream, how extravagantly you labor to possess All, and as long as the frenzy lasts, you do possess that All, you equal God, though no one realizes it, not even God, not even you. The delirium of the poor is the generator of events, the source of history: a throng of hysterics who want another world, here and now. It is they who inspire utopias, it is for them that utopias are written. But *utopia*, let us remember, means *nowhere*.

And *where* would these cities be that evil never touches, in which labor is blessed and death is never feared? There one is constrained to a felicity of geometric idylls, of adjusted ecstasies, of a thousand disgusting wonders necessarily offered by the spectacle of a *perfect* world, a fabricated world. In ludicrous detail, Campanella tells us about the Solarians exempt from "gout, rheumatism, catarrh, sciatica, colic, hydropsy flatus. . . ." Everything abounds in the *City of the Sun* "because each man is eager to distinguish himself in what he does. The leader who presides over each thing is called: *King*. . . . Women and men, divided into bands, go about their work without ever infringing the orders of their *kings*, and without ever appearing fatigued, as we do. They regard their leaders as fathers or as older brothers." We shall recognize the same twaddle in other works of the genre, particularly in those of a Cabet, a Fourier, or a Morris, all lacking in that touch of rancor so necessary to literary works, and not only those.

To conceive a *true* utopia, to sketch, with conviction, the structure of an ideal society, requires a certain dose of ingenuousness, even of stupidity, which, being too evident, ultimately exasperates the reader. The only readable utopias are the false ones, the ones that, written in a spirit of entertainment or misanthropy, prefigure or recall *Gulliver's Travels*, that Bible of the disabused, quintessence of nonchimerical visions, a utopia *without hope*. By his sarcasms, Swift undeceived a genre to the point of destroying it.

Is it easier to confect a utopia than an apocalypse? Both have their principles and their stereotypes. The former, whose clichés are closer to our deepest instincts, has given rise to a much more abundant literature than the latter. Not everyone can reckon with a cosmic catastrophe or love the language and the style with which it is heralded and proclaimed.

But he who acknowledges and applauds such an idea will read, in the Gospels, with all the enthusiasm of vice, the figures and banalities that will prosper on Patmos: "The stars of heaven shall fall unto the earth, and the moon become as blood . . . all the tribes of the earth shall lament . . . nor shall this generation perish before all these things are come to pass." This presentiment of the incredible, of a capital event, this crucial expectation can turn into an illusion, which will be the hope of a paradise on earth or elsewhere; or else it can turn into anxiety, and this will be the vision of an ideal Worst, a voluptuously dreaded cataclysm.

"And out of his mouth goeth a sharp sword, that with it he should smite the nations." Conventions of horror, routine procedures. Saint John had to go in for them, once he opted for that splendid gibberish, that procession of downfalls preferable, all things considered, to the descriptions of cities and islands where you are smothered by an impersonal bliss, where "universal harmony" crushes you in its embrace. The dreams of utopia have for the most part been realized, but in an entirely different spirit from the one in which they had been conceived; what was perfection for utopia is for us a flaw; its chimeras are our disasters. The type of society conceived by utopia in a lyrical tonality seems to us, in operation, intolerable. Judge from the following sample of Cabet's *Voyage en Icarie*: "Two-thousand five-hundred young women (dressmakers) work in a factory, some sitting, some standing, almost all charming. . . . The rule that each worker produces the same object doubles the rapidity of the manufacture and brings it to perfection as well. Thousands of items of the most elegant headware are created each morning by the hands of these lovely workers." Such lucubrations proceed from mental debility or bad taste. And yet Cabet has, in material terms, seen quite accurately; he is mistaken only with regard to the essential. Utterly uninstructed as to the interval that separates *being* and *producing* (we exist, in the full sense of the word, only outside of what we do, only beyond our actions), he could not discern the fatality attached to every form of labor, artisanal, industrial, or otherwise. What is most striking in utopian narratives is the absence of perspicacity, of psychological instinct. Their characters are automatons, fictions or symbols: none is real, none exceeds its puppet status, an idea lost in a universe without reference points. Even the children become unrecognizable. In Fourier's "societary state," they are so pure that they are utterly unaware of the temptation to steal, to "pick an apple off a tree." But a child who does not steal is not a child. What is the use of creating a society of marionettes? I recommend the description of the phalanstery as the most effective vomitive I know.

Placed at the antipodes of a La Rochefoucauld, the inventor of utopias is a moralist who perceives in us only disinterest, craving for sacrifice, self-effacement. Bloodless, perfect, and nil, thunderstruck by Good, stripped of sins and vices, with neither depth nor contour, utterly uninitiated into existence, into the art of embarrassment, of varying one's shames and torments, such men never suspect the pleasure that our neighbor's despair provokes in us, the impatience with which we anticipate and follow his downfall. This impatience and this pleasure can, on occasion, proceed from a proper curiosity, with nothing diabolical about it. As long as someone rises in the world, we do not know who he is, for—his ascent distancing him from himself—he lacks reality, he does not exist. Similarly, we know ourselves only from the moment when we begin to fail, when any success, on the level of human interests, turns out to be impossible: a perspicuous defeat by which, taking possession of our own being, we stand apart from the universal torpor. The better to grasp your own collapse or another's, you must pass through evil and, if need be, plunge deep within it: how manage this in those islands and cities from which it is excluded by principle, by *raison d'état*? Here all shadows are forbidden; only light is admitted. No trace of dualism: utopia is by essence anti-Manichean. Hostile to anomaly, to deformity, to irregularity, it tends to the affirmation of the homogeneous, of the typical, of repetition and orthodoxy. But life is rupture, heresy, derogation from the norms of matter. And man, in relation to life, is heresy to the second degree, victory of the individual, of whim, aberrant apparition, a schismatic animal that society—the totality of sleeping monsters—seeks to recall to the *straight and narrow path*. Heretic par excellence, the wakened monster, an incarnate solitude, infraction of the universal order, delights in his exception, isolates himself in his onerous privileges, and it is in *duration* that he pays for what he gains over his "kind": the more he distinguishes himself from them, the more dangerous and simultaneously the more fragile he will be, for it is at the cost of his longevity that he disturbs the others' peace and that he creates for himself, there in the heart of the city, an *undesirable* standing.

"Our hopes for the future state of the human race can be reduced to these three important points: the destruction of inequality among nations, the progress of equality within one and the same people, and finally the perfecting of humanity." (Condorcet)

Committed to the description of *real* cities, history, which always and everywhere asseverates the failure rather than the fulfillment of our hopes, has ratified none of these forecasts. For a Tactitus, there is no *ideal* Rome. By banishing the irrational and the irreparable, utopia further sets itself against tragedy, paroxysm and quintessence of history. In a perfect city, all conflict would cease; human wills would be throttled, mollified, or rendered miraculously convergent; here would reign only unity, without the ingredient of chance or contradiction. Utopia is a mixture of childish rationalism and secularized angelism.

We are submerged in evil. Not that all our actions are bad; but, when we happen to commit *good* ones, we suffer from them, for having thwarted our spontaneous impulses: the practice of virtue comes down to an exercise of penitence, an apprenticeship to maceration. Fallen angel transformed into a demiurge assigned to Creation, Satan rebels against God and reveals himself, here below, more at ease and even more powerful than He; far from being a usurper, he is our master, a legitimate sovereign who would prevail over the Most High, if the universe were reduced to man. So let us have the courage to acknowledge whom we are responsible to.

The great religions have not been deceived: what Mara offers to Buddha, Ahriman to Zoroaster, the Tempter to Jesus, is the earth and supremacy over the earth, realities well within the power of the Prince of this world. And we are playing his game, cooperating in his enterprise and fulfilling it when we seek to establish a new realm, a generalized utopia or a universal empire, for what he craves above all is that we embroil ourselves with him and that upon his contact we turn away from the light, from the regret for our old felicity.

Closed for five thousand years, paradise was reopened, according to Saint John Chrysostom, at the moment when Christ expired; the thief could enter it now, followed by Adam, repatriated at last, and by a limited number of the Just who were vegetating in the infernal regions, waiting for "the hour of redemption."

Everything suggests that paradise has been bolted shut again and that it will remain so for a long time to come. No one can force an entrance there: the few privileged characters enjoying the place have doubtless barricaded themselves inside, according to a system whose wonders they could observe on earth. This paradise has a look of being the real one: in the depths of our prostrations we dream of it and in it long to dissolve. A sudden impulse leads us to it, and we plunge in: do we seek to regain, in a moment, what we have lost forever—suddenly to make up for the sin of being born? Nothing shows more clearly the metaphysical meaning of our nostalgia than its incapacity to coincide with any moment of time whatever; hence it seeks consolation in a remote, immemorial past refractory to the centuries and somehow anterior to becoming. The evil from which our nostalgia suffers—effect of a rupture that dates back to the beginnings—keeps it from projecting the Age of Gold into the future; the golden age it conceives quite naturally is the old one, the primordial one to which it aspires less for pleasure's sake than to swoon there, to lay down the burden of consciousness. If we return to the source of all seasons, of time itself, it is to rediscover the true paradise there, object of all our regrets. On the other hand, the nostalgia from which the earthly paradise derives will be minus precisely the dimension of regret: a nostalgia reversed, falsified, and vitiated, straining toward the future, obnubilated by "progress," a temporal rejoinder, a jeering metamorphosis of the original paradise. Contagion? Automatism? This metamorphosis has ultimately come to pass within each of us. Willy-nilly we bet on the future, make it into a panacea, and identifying it with the appearance of an altogether *different time* within time, we consider it as an inexhaustible and yet completed duration, a *timeless history*. A contradiction in terms, inherent in the hope of a new kingdom, of a victory of the unsolvable at the heart of becoming. Our dreams of a better world are based on a theoretical impossibility. Hardly surprising if, in order to justify them, we must resort to *solid* paradoxes!

As long as Christianity satisfied men's minds, utopia could not seduce them; once Christianity began to disappoint them, utopia sought to conquer them and to establish itself there. It was already hard at work during the Renaissance, but was not to succeed until two centuries later, in an age of "enlightened" superstitions. Thus was born the Future, vision of an irrevocable happiness, of a maneuvered paradise in which chance has no place, in which the merest fantasy seems like a heresy or a provocation. To describe such a thing would be to enter into the details of the unimaginable. The very notion of an ideal city is a torment to reason, an enterprise that does honor to the heart and disqualifies the intellect. (How could a Plato condescend to such a thing? He is the ancestor, I was forgetting, of all these aberrations, revived and aggravated by Thomas More, the *founder* of modern illusions.) To construct a society where, according to a terrifying ceremony, our acts are catalogued and regulated, where, by a charity carried to the point of indecency, our innermost thoughts are inspected, is to transfer the pangs of hell to the Age of Gold, or to create, with the devil's help, a philanthropic institution. Solarians, Utopians, Harmonians—their hideous names resemble their fate, a nightmare promised to us as well, since we ourselves have erected it into an ideal.

In preaching the advantages of labor, utopias would take the opposite tack from Genesis. On this point especially, they are the expression of a humanity engulfed in toil, proud of conniving with the consequences of the Fall, of which the gravest remains the obsession with profit. The stigmata of a race that cherishes "the sweat of the brow" and makes it a sign of nobility, that labors *exultantly*—these we bear with pride and ostentation; whence the horror inspired in us, reprobates as we are, by the elect who refuse to toil or to excel in any realm whatever. The refusal we reproach them for is one that only the man who preserves the memory of an immemorial happiness is capable of. Alienated among his kind, he is like them and yet cannot communicate with them; whichever way he looks, he does not feel he is *from hereabouts*; whatever he discerns seems to him a usurpation: the very fact of bearing a name . . . His enterprises fail, he ventures upon them without believing in them: simulacra from which the *precise* image of another world alienates him. Man, once expelled from paradise, in order not to think about it anymore, in order not to suffer from it, is given in compensation the faculty of will, of aspiring to action, of foundering there with enthusiasm, with brio. . . . But the abulic, in his detachment, in his supernatural marasmus— what effort can he make, to what goal can he abandon himself? Nothing induces him to emerge from his . . . absence. And yet he himself does not entirely escape the common curse: he *exhausts himself* in a regret and expends on it more energy than we deploy in all our exploits.

When Christ promised that the "kingdom of God" was neither "here" nor "there," but within us, he doomed in advance the utopian constructions for which any "kingdom" is necessarily *exterior*, with no relation to our inmost self or our individual salvation. So deeply have utopias marked us, that it is from outside, from the course of events or from the progress of collectivities that we await our deliverance. Thus was devised the Meaning of history, whose vogue would supplant that of Progress, without adding anything new to it. Yet it was necessary to shelve not a concept, but one of its verbal translations, which had been abused. In ideological matters, we are not easily renewed without the help of synonyms.

Various as are its disguises, the notion of perfectibility has made its way into our manners: to it subscribes even the man who questions it. That history just unfolds, independently of a specified direction, of a goal, no one is willing to admit. "A Goal—surely it has one, races toward it, has all but reached it," proclaim our doctrines and our desires. The more heavily an idea is burdened with immediate promises, the greater likelihood it has of triumphing. Unable to find "the kingdom of God" within themselves, or rather too cunning to want to seek it there, Christians placed it in the course of events—in becoming: they perverted a teaching in order to ensure its success. Furthermore, Christ himself sustained the ambiguity; on one hand, answering the insinuations of the Pharisees, he recommended an interior kingdom, remote from time; and on the other he signified to his disciples that, salvation being imminent, they and the "present generation" would witness the consummation of all things. Having understood that human beings accept martyrdom for a chimera but not for a truth, he came to terms with their weakness. Had he acted otherwise, he would have compromised his work. But what in him was concession or tactic is in the utopianists postulate or passion.

A great step forward was made the day men understood that, in order to torment one another more effectively, they would have to gather together, to organize themselves into a society. If we are to believe the utopias, they succeeded in doing so only by halves; the utopias therefore offer to help them, to furnish them a context appropriate to the exercise of a complete happiness, while requiring, in return, that men abdicate their freedom or, if they retain it, that they use it solely to proclaim their joy amid the sufferings they inflict upon each other. Such seems the meaning of the infernal solicitude the utopias show toward men. Under these conditions, how can we fail to envisage a reverse utopia, a liquidation of the infinitesimal good and the enormous evil attached to the existence of any social order whatever? The project is alluring, the temptation irresistible. How put an end to so vast an amount of anomalies? It would require something comparable to the *universal dissolvent* sought by the alchemists and whose efficacy would be tested not on metals but on institutions. Until the formula is found, let us note in passing that in their positive aspects, alchemy and utopia coincide: pursuing, in heterogeneous realms, a dream of transmutation that is related if not identical, one attacks the irreducible in nature, the other the irreducible in history. And it is from one and the same spiritual vice, or from one and the same hope, that the elixir of life and the ideal city derive.

Just as a nation, in order to set itself apart from the others, in order to humiliate and overwhelm them, or simply in order to acquire a unique physiognomy, needs an extrava-

gant idea to guide it, to propose goals incommensurable
with its real capacities, so a society evolves and asserts itself
only if ideals are suggested to it, or inculcated in it, out of
all proportion to what it is. Utopia fulfills, in the life of
collectivities, the function assigned to the notion of "mission" in the life of peoples. Hence ideologies are the by-
product and, in a sense, the vulgar expression of messianic
or utopian visions.

In itself an ideology is neither good nor bad. Everything
depends on the moment when it is adopted. Communism,
for example, acts upon a virile nation like a stimulant; it
impels it onward and favors its expansion; on a tottering
nation, its influence may be less happy. Neither true nor
false, it precipitates matters, and it is not *because* of it but
through it that Russia acquired its present vigor. Would it
play the same part, once established throughout the rest of
Europe? Would it be a principle of renewal? One would
like to hope so; in any case, the question admits of only an
indirect, an arbitrary answer, inspired by analogies of a historical order. Let us reflect upon the effects of Christianity
at its beginnings: it delivered a fatal blow to ancient society,
paralyzed it, finished it off; on the other hand, it was a
blessing to the Barbarians, whose instincts were enhanced
upon contact. Far from regenerating a decrepit world, it
regenerated only the regenerated. In the same fashion, communism will bring about, *in the immediate future*, the salvation of only those who are already saved; it cannot provide
a concrete hope to the moribund, still less can it reanimate
corpses.

After having denounced the absurdities of utopia, let us
deal with its merits, and, since men accommodate social
arrangements so well and scarcely distinguish from them the

evils immanent within them, let us do as they do, let us unite ourselves with their unconsciousness.

We shall never praise the utopias sufficiently for having denounced the crimes of ownership, the horror property represents, the calamities it causes. Great or small, the owner is corrupted, sullied in his essence: his corruption is projected onto the merest object he touches or appropriates. Whether his "fortune" is threatened or stripped from him, he will be compelled to a consciousness of which he is normally incapable. In order to reassume a human appearance, in order to regain his "soul," he must be ruined and must consent to his ruin. In this, the revolution will help him. By restoring him to his primal nakedness, it annihilates him in the immediate future and saves him in the absolute, for it liberates—inwardly, it is understood—those whom it strikes first: the haves; it *reclassifies* them, it restores to them their former dimension and leads them back to the values they have betrayed. But even before having the means or the occasion to strike them, the revolution sustains in them a salutary fear: it troubles their sleep, nourishes their nightmares, and nightmare is the beginning of a metaphysical awakening. Hence it is as an agent of destruction that the revolution is seen to be useful; however deadly, one thing always redeems it: it alone knows what kind of terror to use in order to shake up this world of owners, the cruelest of all possible worlds. Every form of possession, let us not hesitate to insist, degrades, debases, flatters the monster sleeping deep within each of us. To own even a broom, to count anything at all as *our* property, is to participate in the general infamy. What pride to discover that nothing belongs to you—what a revelation! You took yourself for the last of men, and now, suddenly, astonished and virtually enlightened by your destitution, you no longer suffer from it; quite the contrary, you pride yourself in it. And all you still desire is to be as indigent as a saint or a madman.

When we are exasperated by traditional values, we necessarily orient ourselves toward the ideology that denies them. And it is by its force of negation that utopia seduces, much more than by its positive formulas. To desire the overthrow of the social order is to pass through a crisis more or less marked by communist themes. This is true today, as it was true yesterday and will be true even tomorrow. Everything suggests that, since the Renaissance, men's minds have been attracted on the surface by liberalism, and in depth by communism, which, far from being a product of circumstances, a historical accident, is the heir of utopian systems and the beneficiary of a long subterranean labor; initially a caprice or a schism, it was ultimately to assume the character of a destiny and an orthodoxy. At the present time, our consciousness can waken to only two forms of revolt: communist and anticommunist. Yet how can we fail to realize that anticommunism is equivalent to a furious, horrified faith in the future of communism?

When an ideology's moment has come, everything contributes to its success, even its enemies; neither polemics nor police can check its expansion or delay its success; it seeks, and it is able, to realize itself, to incarnate itself; but the better it succeeds, the greater risk it runs of exhausting itself; once established, it will be drained of its ideal content, will extenuate its resources, compromising the promises of salvation it possessed, only to degenerate at the end into a bugbear or humbug.

The career reserved for communism depends on the rate

at which it expends its utopian reserves. So long as it possesses them, it will inevitably tempt all societies that have not experienced such a thing; retreating here, advancing there, invested with virtues no other ideology possesses, it will circle the earth, replacing defunct or declining religions, and everywhere offering the modern crowd an absolute worthy of its nothingness.

Considered in itself, communism appears as the only reality to which one might still subscribe, if one harbors even a wisp of illusion as to the future: this is why, to various degrees, we are all communists. . . . But is it not a sterile speculation to judge a doctrine apart from the anomalies inherent in its practical realization? Man will always anticipate the advent of justice; for justice to triumph, he will renounce freedom, which he will afterward regret. Whatever he undertakes, this impasse haunts his actions and his thoughts, as if it were not its final term but its point of departure, its condition, and its key. No new social form is in a position to safeguard the advantages of the old: a virtually equal amount of disadvantages is encountered in all types of society. A cursed equilibrium, an irremediable stagnation, from which individuals and collectivities suffer alike. Theories can do nothing about it, the depths of history being impermeable to the doctrines that mark its appearance. The Christian era was quite a different thing from Christianity; the communist era, in its turn, cannot evoke communism as such. There exists no event that is naturally Christian, or naturally communist.

If utopia was illusion hypostasized, communism, going still further, will be illusion decreed, imposed: a challenge to the omnipresence of evil, an *obligatory* optimism. A man will find it hard to accommodate himself to it if he lives, by dint of ordeals and experiments, in the intoxication of disappointment and if, like the author of Genesis, he is reluctant to identify the Age of Gold with the future, with becoming. Not that he scorns the fanatics of "infinite progress" and their efforts to make justice prevail here on earth; but he knows, to his misery, that justice is a material impossibility, a grandiose meaninglessness, the only ideal about which we can declare quite certainly that it will never be realized, and against which nature and society seem to have mobilized all their laws.

These factions, these conflicts are not uniquely those of a solitary. With more or less intensity, we too endure them, all the rest of us: are we not at the point of longing for the destruction of this very society, even while knowing the misadventures reserved for us by the one that will replace it? A total overthrow, however useless, a revolution *without faith* is all we can still hope for from a period in which no one is sufficiently honest to be a true revolutionary. When, tormented by the frenzy of the intellect, we give ourselves up to that of chaos, we react like a madman in possession of his faculties, a lunatic superior to his lunacy, or like a god who, in a fit of lucid rage, delights in pulverizing his work and his being.

Our dreams of the future are henceforth inseparable from our fears. Utopian literature, at its beginnings, rebelled against the Middle Ages, against the high esteem in which they held Hell and against the taste they professed for doomsday visions. It seems as if the reassuring systems of a Campanella or a More were conceived with the sole purpose of discrediting the hallucinations of a Saint Hildegarde. Today, reconciled with the terrible, we are seeing a contamination of utopia by apocalypse: the heralded "new earth" increasingly assumes the aspect of a new Hell. But this Hell is one we are waiting for, we even make it a duty to precipitate its advent. The two genres, utopian and apocalyptic, which once seemed so dissimilar to us, interpenetrate, rub off on each other, to form a third, wonderfully apt to reflect the kind of reality that threatens us and to which we shall nonetheless assent with a correct and disabused yes. That will be our way of being *irreproachable* in the face of fatality.

The Golden Age

===

I

"In those days, men lived like gods, free of care, knowing
neither labor nor pain. Old age and its miseries never visited
them, and retaining the strength of their hands and limbs
as long as they lived, they feasted in delight, shielded from
all harm. Men died as if they fell asleep, overcome by no
more than drowsiness. Every good was theirs; the fertile
land afforded plentiful nourishment of itself, and men ate
and drank at their pleasure. . . ."

Hesiod's portrait of the golden age matches that of the
biblical Eden. One is as conventional as the other: unreality
cannot be dramatic. At least they share the merit of defining
the image of a static world where identity ceaselessly con-
templates itself, ruled by an eternal present, that tense common to all visions of paradise, a time forged in opposition
to the very idea of time. In order to conceive and aspire to
it, we must execrate all becoming, having endured its weight,
its calamity; we must long to wrest ourselves free of it at
any cost. This longing is the only one a feeble will is capable
of, a will eager to rest, to dissolve . . . elsewhere. Had we
adhered without reservation to the eternal present, history

would not have occurred, or in any case would not have been synonymous with burden, with torment. When it weighs too heavily upon us, when it overwhelms us, a nameless cowardice seizes upon our being: the prospect of further struggles among the centuries assumes nightmare proportions. The accommodations of that mythological age allure us then to the point of pain, or if we have frequented Genesis, the divagations of regret transplant us into the happy stupors of the first garden, while our mind evokes the angels and turns itself inside out to penetrate their secret. The more we think about them, the higher they rise out of our lassitude, not without some advantage to ourselves: do they not permit us to appreciate the degree of our inaptitude for the world, of our awkwardness in getting ourselves into it? However impalpable, however unreal they may be, yet they are less so than we who brood upon them and invoke them, shadows or counterfeit shadows, desiccated flesh, annihilated breath. And it is with all our wretchedness, as oppressed ghosts, that we ponder them, beseeching. . . . There is nothing "terrible" in their nature, as a certain elegy claims; no, what is terrible is to have reached the point of being able to deal with nothing but them, or, when we suppose them a thousand miles away from us, suddenly to see them emerging from the twilight of our own flesh and blood.

II

As for the "sources of life," which the gods, according to Hesiod again, have hidden from us, it was Prometheus who took it upon himself to reveal them. Responsible for all our misfortunes, he was quite unaware of being so, though he

prided himself in his lucidity. The remarks Aeschylus puts
in his mouth are word for word the contrary of those we
have just read in *Works and Days*: "In those days, men saw,
but saw badly; they listened, but failed to understand. . . . They took action, but never realized what they
were doing." We recognize the tone—no use quoting any
further. What Prometheus reproached men for, after all,
was their plunge into the primordial idyll, their conformity
to the laws of their nature, unbroached by consciousness.
By wakening them to mind, by separating them from those
"sources" they had previously enjoyed without attempting
to sound their depths or their significance, he brought them
not happiness but the curse and the torments of titanism.
They were doing very well without consciousness; he came
to inflict it upon them, to nail them to it, and consciousness
provoked within them a drama which extends to each of us
and will end only with the race itself. With every passing
day, consciousness gains a greater hold over us, dominates
us, tears us away from life; we try clinging to life anew and,
failing, turn against life and consciousness both, then we
weigh their meaning and their données, until, exasperated,
we turn against ourselves. This he had not anticipated, our
deadly philanthropist whose sole excuse was illusion, a tempter
in spite of himself, a feckless and blundering serpent. Men
listened; what need did they have to *understand*? Prometheus
obliged them to do so, handing them over to becoming, to
history; in other words, driving them out of the eternal
present. Innocent or guilty, what does it matter: Prometheus
deserved his punishment.

The first zealot of "science," a *modern* in the worst sense
of the word, his heroics and his ravings herald those of many
a doctrinaire of the last century: only his sufferings console

us for so many extravagances. Now that eagle—there is someone who *understood* and who, divining our future, sought to spare us its horrors. But the machine had been started: men had already acquired a taste for the wiles of the seducer who, modeling them in his own image, taught them to rummage, like himself, in the *underside* of life, despite the prohibition of the gods. Prometheus is the instigator of all the indiscretions and misdemeanors of knowledge, the source of that murderous curiosity which keeps us from marrying the world: by idealizing knowledge and action, did he not thereby ruin Being, and with Being, the possibility of the golden age? The tribulations to which he doomed us, if not equal to his, would nonetheless last longer. His "program," coherent as fatality, he realized to perfection, only in reverse; everything he preached to us, everything he imposed upon us has turned point by point first against him, then against us. One does not shake off original unconsciousness with impunity; those who, following his lead, cast aspersions upon it inexorably suffer his fate: they are devoured, they too have their rock and their eagle. And the hatred with which they thank him is all the more virulent in that they hate themselves *in him*.

III

The transition of the silver age, then to that of bronze and of iron, marks the progress of our downfall, of our alienation from that eternal present of which we conceive no more than a simulacrum and with which we have ceased to have a common frontier: it belongs to another universe, it eludes us, and we are so distinct from it that we barely succeed in suspecting its nature. No way of appropriating it: did we ever really possess it? And how regain our footing there when nothing restores its image in us, for us? We are forever thwarted, and if we ever do approach it, the merit of our success goes to those extremities of satiety and sluggishness wherein it is, however, no more than a caricature of itself, a parody of the immutable, a prostrate becoming frozen in a timeless avarice, huddled over a sterile moment, over a treasure which impoverishes it—a spectral becoming, powerless and yet fulfilled, stuffed as it is with the void. For beings to whom ecstasy was forbidden, no glimpse of origin, save by the extinction of their vitality, by the absence of any attribute, by that sensation of hollow infinity, of a cheapened abyss, of inflated space and of a suppliant, spoiled duration.

There is an authentic, positive eternity, which extends beyond time; there is another one, negative and false, located within it: that eternity in which we stagnate, far from salvation, outside the competence of any redeemer, and which liberates us from everything by depriving us of everything. The universe impoverished, we exhaust ourselves in the spectacle of our own appearances. Has it atrophied, then, the organ that once allowed us to perceive the depths of our being? And are we forever reduced to our semblances? When a list is someday made of all the ills the flesh and spirit are heir to, they will still be as nothing to the one that comes from our incapacity to marry ourselves to the eternal present, or to steal from it, for our delight, even the tiniest fraction.

Fallen without recourse into a negative eternity, into that scattered time which affirms itself only by annulling itself, an essence reduced to a series of destructions, a summa of ambiguities, a plenitude whose principle abides in the void, we live and die in each of its moments without knowing *when* it is, for in truth it *never* is. For all its precariousness, we are so attached to it that in order to tear ourselves from it, we require more than an eruption of our habits: a lesion of the mind, a crack in the self, through which we might glimpse the indestructible and gain access to it, a favor granted only to certain reprobates in recompense for their assent to their own destruction. The rest—the great majority of mortals, while avowing their incapacity for such a sacrifice, never renounce the quest for *another* time; they devote themselves to it, on the contrary, with desperation, but locate it here on earth, according to the prescriptions of utopia, which seek to reconcile the eternal present with history, the delights of the golden age with Promethean ambitions, or, to resort to biblical terminology, to remake Eden with the instruments of the Fall, thereby permitting the new Adam to know the advantages of the old one. Is this not to attempt to revise the Creation?

IV

Vico's notion of constructing an "ideal history" and of tracing its "eternal circle" is recognizable, applied to society, in the utopian systems characterized by their effort to solve the "social question" once and for all. Whence their obsession with the *definitive* and their impatience to institute paradise as soon as possible, in the immediate future, a kind of stationary duration, an immobilized Possible, a counterfeit of the eternal present. "If I prophesy," says Fourier, "so unhesitatingly the universal harmony as an imminent phe-

nomenon, it is because the organization of the societary state
requires no more than two years. . . ." A naïve avowal if
ever there was one, which betrays, nonetheless, a profound
reality. Would we fling ourselves into even the flimsiest
enterprise without the secret conviction that the absolute
depends upon us, our ideas, our actions, and that we can
guarantee their triumph in a short period of time? Any man
who identifies himself completely with something behaves
as if he were anticipating the advent of "the universal harmony," or considered himself its promoter. To act is to
anchor in an imminent future, so imminent it becomes almost tangible; to act is to feel you are consubstantial with
that future. Which is not the case for those persecuted by
the demon of procrastination. "What can be usefully post-
poned can be even more usefully abandoned," they repeat
with Epictetus, though their passion for postponement does
not proceed, as it does for the Stoic, from any moral consideration, but from an almost methodical dread and from
a disgust too inveterate not to assume the qualities of a
discipline or a vice. If they have proscribed the before and
the after, evacuated today and tomorrow as equally unin-
habitable, it is because it is easier for them to live in imagination ten thousand years hence than to loll in the immediate
and the imminent. With the years, they will have thought
more about time-in-itself than time passing, more about the
indefinite than the effective, more about the end of the
world than the end of a day. Knowing duration neither in
the extent of moments nor in privileged sites, they move
from failure to failure, and when even this progress is pro-
hibited, they stop, look in every direction, question the
horizon: there is no more horizon. . . . And that is when
they experience not vertigo but panic, a panic so powerful

that it erases their steps and prevents them from escaping. They are men excluded, banished, men outlawed from time, disjointed from the rhythm that sweeps on the mob, men victimized by an anemic and lucid will, struggling with itself, endlessly *listening to itself.* To will, in the fullest sense of the word, is to be unaware that one wills, is to refuse to loiter over the phenomenon of the will. The man of action weighs neither his impulses nor his motives, still less does he consult his reflexes: he obeys them without reflecting upon them, and without hampering them. It is not action in itself that interests him but its goal, its intention; similarly, the *object* will attract him, and not the mechanism of the will. At grips with the world, he seeks what is definitive in it or hopes to put it there himself, right now or in two years. . . . To manifest oneself is to let oneself be blinded by some form or other of perfection: not even movement *as such* fails to contain a utopian ingredient. Even to breathe would be a torture without the memory or anticipation of paradise, supreme—and yet unconscious—object of our desires, unformulated essence of our memory and our expectation. Incapable of divulging it in the subsoil of their nature, too hurried as well to be able to dig it out, we moderns must project it into the future, and the epigraph of the Saint-Simonian journal *Le Producteur* represents the shortcut of all our illusions: "The golden age, which a blind tradition located in the past, lies before us." Hence we are eager to hasten its advent, to institute it for eternity, according to an eschatology deriving not from anxiety but from exaltation and euphoria, from a suspect and almost morbid greed for happiness. The revolutionary thinks that the overthrow he is preparing will be the last; all of us think the same thing in the sphere of our activities: *the ultimate* is the obsession of the living. We bestir ourselves because it is up to us, we think, to complete history, to close it, because it appears to us as our domain, as does "truth" itself, emerging at last from its chaste reserve to reveal itself. Error will be the fate of others; only we shall have understood everything. Victor over his kind, then over God, seeking to revise His work, to correct its imperfections—anyone who has not tried as much, who does not believe it is his duty to try, renounces his own destiny, whether out of wisdom or weakness. Prometheus sought to do better than Zeus; improvised demiurges, each of us tries to do better than God, to inflict upon Him the humiliation of a paradise superior to His, to suppress the irreparable, to "defatalize" the world, borrowing a word from Proudhon's jargon. In its general outline, utopia is a cosmogonic dream *on the level of history*.

V

We shall not build paradise here on earth so long as men are marked by Sin; hence we must release them from it, liberate them. The systems that have been committed to doing so participate in a more or less disguised Pelagianism. Pelagius (a Celt, a naïf), by denying the effects of the Fall, deprived Adam's lie of any power to affect posterity. Our first ancestor lived a strictly personal drama, incurred a disgrace that regarded him alone, without in any way knowing the pleasure of bequeathing to us his flaws and misfortunes. Born good and free, there is in us no trace of an original corruption.

It is hard to imagine a doctrine more generous and more untrue; this is a heresy of the utopian type, fruitful by its very extravagances, by its absurdities which were rich in *futures*. Not that the authors of utopias took their inspiration from it directly; but it is incontestable that in modern thought there exists, hostile to Augustinianism and to Jansenism, an authentic current of Pelagianism—the idolatry of progress and all revolutionary ideologies will be its conclusion—according to which we constitute a mass of the *virtual* elect, emancipated from original sin, infinitely malleable, predestined to the good, capable of any and every perfection. Robert Owen's manifesto promises us a system capable of creating "a *new* spirit and a *new* will in the entire human race, and thereby to lead each man, by an irresistible necessity, to become consistent, rational, healthy in judgment and in conduct."

Pelagius, like his remote disciples, starts from a fiercely optimistic vision of our nature. But there is no proof of any kind that the will is *good*; it is even certain that it is anything but, the new will equally with the old. Only men with a deficient will are spontaneously good; the others must apply themselves to being so, and succeed only at the cost of efforts that embitter them. Evil being inseparable from action, the consequence is that our undertakings are necessarily directed *against* someone or something; at the limit, against ourselves. But usually, I must insist, we *will* only at someone else's expense. Far from being more or less elect, we are more or less reprobates. If you want to construct a society in which men do no harm to one another, you must admit only abulics.

What we have is more than the choice between a sick will and a bad one; the former excellent because stricken, immobilized, ineffectual; the latter noxious and hence active, invested by a dynamic principle: the very one that sustains the fever of becoming and provokes *events*. Take it away from man, if you want a golden age! Which would be as much as to strip him of his very being, whose entire secret resides in that propensity to do harm, without which he is inconceivable. Resistant to his own happiness and to that of others, he acts as if he longed for the institution of an ideal society; if it were achieved, he would smother in it, the disadvantages of satiety being incomparably greater than those of poverty. He loves tension, perpetual advance: toward what would make his way within perfection? Unfit for the eternal present, he dreads moreover its monotony, that reef of paradise in its double form: religious and utopian. Isn't history ultimately the result of our fear of boredom, of that fear which will always make us cherish the novelty and the spice of disaster, and prefer any misfortune to stagnation? An obsession with the unheard-of is the destructive principle of our salvation. We head for hell to the degree that we leave the vegetative life behind, that life whose passivity would constitute the key to everything, the supreme answer to all our questions; the horror it inspires in us has made us into that horde of civilized men, of omniscient monsters who know nothing of the essential. To be bored in slow motion, to endure with dignity the injustice of Being, to wrest ourselves away from expectation, from the oppression of hope, to seek a middle term between breathing and the corpse—we are all too corrupted and too winded for that. There is no help for it: nothing will reconcile us with boredom. Were we less rebellious to its sway, we should know, by some succor from on high, a plenitude without events, the pleasure of the invariable instant, the delectation of identity. But such a grace is so contrary to our nature that we are only too happy not to receive it.

Riven to diversity, we mine it for that constant quantity of excesses and conflicts so necessary to our instincts. Released from care and from all shackles, we should be delivered to ourselves; the vertigo we would suffer then would leave us a thousand times worse off than our servitude does. This aspect of our failure escaped the anarchists, the last Pelagians to date, who nonetheless were superior to their predecessors in that they rejected, in their cult of freedom, every city, beginning with the "ideal" ones, and substituted for them a new variety of chimeras, more brilliant and more improbable than the old. If they raged against the State and demanded its suppression, it was because they saw it as an obstacle to the exercise of a will that was fundamentally good; now, it is precisely because the will is bad, is wicked, that the State was born; if the State were to vanish, the will would give itself up to evil without any restriction whatever. Nonetheless, the anarchists' idea of annihilating all authority remains one of the finest ever conceived. And we can never sufficiently deplore the fact that the race of those who sought to realize it is now extinct. But perhaps they had to fade, to absent themselves from an age like ours, so eager to invalidate their theories and their prophecies. They heralded the era of the individual: the individual is drawing to his close; they proclaimed the eclipse of the State: the State was never stronger or more oppressive; they hailed the age of equality: it is the age of terror which has come. Everything runs down. Compared to theirs, even our crimes have deteriorated in quality: those we now and then still deign to commit lack that atmosphere of the absolute which redeemed theirs, always executed with so much care and so much brio! Is there anyone today willing to throw bombs for the establishment of "the universal harmony," a capital fiction from which we no longer expect anything at all? Besides, what could we hope from it, at the end of the iron age we have come to? The prevailing sentiment now is disillusion, the summa of our tainted dreams. And if we have not even the resource of believing in the virtues of destruction, it is because we are all secularized anarchists today and have understood not only their urgency but also their uselessness.

VI

Suffering, in its early stages, counts on the golden age here on earth, seeks a basis for it, attaches itself to it, in a sense; but as suffering intensifies, it withdraws, attached only to itself. Once an accomplice of utopian systems, it now rises against them, discerning in them a mortal danger to the preservation of its own pangs, whose charms it has just discovered. With the voice of Dostoevsky's *Notes from Underground* it will plead in favor of chaos, rise up against reason, against "two and two equals four," against the "crystal palace," that replica of the phalanstery.

He who has glimpsed the inferno, with its hierarchy of woes, will recognize its terrible symmetry in the ideal city, universal happiness, repugnant to anyone who has suffered greatly: Dostoevsky vented his hostility to utopia to the point of intolerance. As he grew older, he was to define himself increasingly by an opposition to the Fourierist notion of his youth: unable to forgive himself for having subscribed to them, he took his revenge upon his own heroes, superhuman . . . caricatures of his first illusions. What he loathed in them were his former divagations, the conces-

sions he had granted to utopia, many of whose themes were
to pursue him nonetheless: when, with the Grand Inquisitor,
he divides humanity into a happy herd and a ravaged, clear-
sighted minority which assumes the destinies of the others;
or when, with Verkhovensky, he tries to make Stavrogin
into the spiritual leader of the future city, an atheist and
revolutionary sovereign pontiff, the novelist takes his inspiration from the "priesthood" the Saint-Simonians set above
the "producers" or from Enfantin's plan to make Saint-Simon
himself the pope of the new religion. Dostoevsky links Catholicism to "socialism," he even identifies them, in a per-
spective that partakes of method and madness equally, an
eminently Slav melange. In relation to the West, everything
in Russia is heightened one degree: skepticism becomes
nihilism; hypothesis, dogma; idea, icon. Shigalev utters no
more lunacies than, say, Cabet, only he goes about it with
an intensity not to be found in his French model. "You have
no obsessions left, only we have any now," the Russians
seem to be telling the West through Dostoevsky, that obsessive par excellence, partisan, like all his characters, of a
single dream: the dream of the golden age, without which,
he assures us, "peoples have no will to live, and cannot even
die." He himself does not expect its realization in history;
on the contrary, he dreads its advent, though without going
over to the "reaction," for he attacks "progress" in the name
not of order but of whim, of the right to caprice. After
having rejected the paradise to come, will he *save* the other
one, the old, the immemorial one? He will make it the
subject of a dream he attributes successively to Stavrogin,
to Versilov, and to "the ridiculous man."

  "In the Dresden Gallery, there is a painting by Claude
Lorrain listed in the catalogue under the title *Acis and Gal-*

atea. . . . It was this picture that I saw in my dream, but not as a picture—as a reality. There was a landscape from the Greek archipelago, just as in the painting, and I seemed to have moved back in time some three thousand years. Blue waves gently lapping, rocks and islets, blossoming shores, and in the distance, an enchanting panorama, the lure of the setting sun. . . . Here was the cradle of humanity. . . . Men woke and fell asleep happy and innocent; the woods rang with their joyous songs, and they expended their abundant powers in making love, in simple pleasures. All this I experienced even as I discerned the enormous future which lay ahead of them, and whose very existence they did not suspect, and my heart shuddered at such thoughts." (*The Possessed*)

Versilov, in his turn, will dream the same dream as Stavrogin, though with this difference, that the setting sun will suddenly appear to him no longer as that of the beginning but as that of the end of "European humanity." In *A Raw Youth*, this picture is somewhat darkened; and altogether darkened in "The Dream of a Ridiculous Man." The golden age and its clichés are presented here with more exactitude and spirit than in the two preceding dreams: a vision of Claude Lorrain annotated by a Sarmatian Hesiod. We are on the earth "before it was tainted by original sin." Men lived there "in a kind of amorous fervor, universal and reciprocal," having children but without knowing the horrors of eroticism and childbirth, wandering through the woods singing hymns and, plunged in a perpetual ecstasy, knowing nothing of jealousy, anger, sickness, and so on. All of which still sounds conventional enough. Fortunately for us, their bliss which seemed eternal was, when put to the test, precarious enough: "the ridiculous man" came among them and

perverted them all. With the appearance of evil, the clichés
vanish, the picture grows livelier: "Like a contagious disease,
an atom of plague capable of contaminating a whole empire,
even so I contaminated by my presence a blissful land innocent until my advent. They learned to lie and delighted
in deceit, they learned the beauty of mendacity. Perhaps all
this began quite innocently, playfully, teasingly, as if it were
a kind of game, and in fact perhaps by means of some atom,
but this atom of lying made its way into their hearts and
they found it good, even lovable. Soon after, voluptuous
pleasure was born, and in turn engendered jealousy, and
jealousy cruelty. . . . Oh, I don't know, I don't remember
any more, but soon, quickly enough, blood was shed in its
first jets and splashes: they were amazed, frightened, and
they began to avoid one another, to separate. Alliances were
formed, but now they were directed against the others. Re-
proaches and castigations were heard. They learned what
shame is, and of shame they made a virtue. The sense of
honor was born among them, and brandished its flag over
each alliance. They began to mistreat the animals, and the
animals left them for the depths of the forests, where they
lived hostile to mankind. An age of struggles began, favoring
separatism, individualism, personality, and the distinction
of mine and thine. There came to pass a diversity of lan-
guages. Men learned sadness and learned even to love it;
they aspired to suffering and said that the truth was to be
had by suffering alone. Having become wicked, it was then
that they began to speak of brotherhood and humanity, and
that they understood such ideas. Having become criminal,
it was then that they invented justice and handed down
codes of law in order to preserve it; then, in order to insure
respect for these codes, they instituted the guillotine. They

had no more than a faint memory of what they had lost, they would not even believe that once they had been innocent and happy. They never tired of deriding the possibility of their former happiness, which they called a dream." (See *A Writer's Diary*.)

But there is worse: they were to discover that consciousness of life is superior to life and the knowledge of the "laws of happiness" superior to happiness. Henceforth, they were lost; by dividing men against themselves by the demoniac work of science, by casting them out of the eternal present and into history, had not "the ridiculous man" reinvented for them the errors and follies of Prometheus?

His crime perpetrated, he begins preaching—at the instigation of remorse—a crusade for the reconquest of this world of delights he has just destroyed. He commits himself to it, but without conviction. Nor is the author convinced either—at least such is our impression: having rejected the formulas of the Future, he turns toward his preferred obsession, toward the age-old felicity, only to expose its inconsistency and its phantasmagoria. Horrified by his discovery, he will try to attenuate its effects, to revive his illusions, to save, if only ideally, his dearest dream. He will not succeed, as he knows, just as we know, and we do injustice to his thought by declaring that it concludes with the *double impossibility of paradise*.

Moreover, is it not revealing that, in order to describe the idyllic landscape of the three versions of the dream, he has resorted to Claude Lorrain, whose insipid delights he so prized, just as Nietzsche did? (What an abyss is supposed by so disconcerting a predilection!) But the moment it is a matter of depicting the disintegration of original felicity, the decor and dizziness of the fall, he borrows nothing from anyone, he mines himself, dismisses any alien suggestion; he even stops imagining and dreaming—he *sees*. And at last he finds himself in his element, at the heart of the iron age, for the love of which he had battled against the "crystal palace" and sacrificed Eden.

VII

When so authoritative a voice has taught us the fragility of the former golden age and the nullity of the future one, we must draw the consequences and no longer let ourselves be deceived by Hesiod's divagations or by those of Prometheus, still less by that synthesis of them the utopias have attempted. Harmony, universal or otherwise, has never existed and never will exist. As for justice, in order to believe it possible, in order even to imagine it, we must have the advantage of a supernatural talent for blindness, of an unprecedented election, a divine grace reinforced by a diabolic one, and count, further, on an effort of generosity from heaven and hell alike, an effort, in truth, highly improbable on the one side as on the other. According to Karl Barth, we could not even "draw a breath of life if, deep within us, there did not exist this certainty: God is just." Yet there are those who still manage to live without knowing that certainty, even without ever having known it. What is their secret, and knowing what they know, by what miracle do they still draw breath?

However pitiless our denials, we never quite destroy the objects of our nostalgia: our dreams survive our waking and our analysis. Though we have stopped believing in the geographical reality of paradise, and in its various figurations, it resides within us nonetheless, a supreme *given*, a dimension of our original ego; now the question is to discover it there. When we succeed, we enter into that glory the theologians call *essential*; but it is not God we see face to face, it is the eternal present, wrested from becoming and from eternity itself. . . . What does history matter from that moment—it is not the seat of being, it is its absence, the *no* of all things, the rupture of the living with themselves; not being kneaded of the same substance as history, we refuse to cooperate any further with its convulsions. Let it crush us, it will affect only our appearances and our impurities, those *vestiges of time* we still drag behind us, symbols of failure, scars of nondeliverance.

The remedy for all our ills must be sought within ourselves, in the timeless principle of our nature. If the unreality of such a principle were proved, we should be lost without hope of appeal. What proof could prevail, however, against the intimate, impassioned conviction that some part of us escapes duration, against the irruption of those moments when God coincides with a clarity suddenly appearing at our limits, a beatitude which projects us far into ourselves, a seizure outside the universe? No more past, no more future; the centuries collapse, matter abdicates, the shadows are exhausted; death turns to ridicule, and ridiculous too is life itself. And this seizure, even if we have experienced it only once, would suffice to reconcile us with all our shames and miseries, of which it is doubtless the recompense. It is as if *all* time had come to visit us, for one final instance, before disappearing. . . . No use retracing the old paradise or racing toward the one to come: the former is inaccessible, the latter unrealizable. What matters, on the other hand, is to internalize nostalgia or expectation, necessarily frustrated when they venture outward, and to constrain them to divulge, or to create within us, the happiness we respectively regret or anticipate. No paradise unless deep within our being, and somehow in the very heart of the self, the self's self; and even here, in order to find it, we must have inspected every paradise, past and possible, have loved and hated them with all the clumsiness of fanaticism, scrutinized and rejected them with the competence of disappointment itself.

Let it be said that we substitute one ghost for another, that the fables of the golden age are well worth the eternal present we dream of, and that the original ego, basis of our hopes, evokes the void and ultimately reduces itself to it. . . . Yet a void that affords plenitude, a fulfilling void—does it not contain more reality than all history possesses from beginning to end?